THE WACKY TOP 40

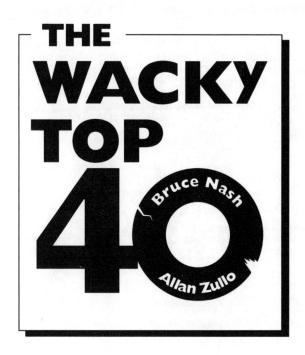

THE WACKY TOP 40

Bruce Nash

Allan Zullo

BOB ADAMS, INC.
PUBLISHERS
Holbrook, Massachusetts

Published by Bob Adams, Inc.
260 Center Street, Holbrook, MA 02343

ISBN: 1-55850-302-1

Printed in the United States of America

A   B   C   D   E   F   G   H   I   J

This publication is designed to provide accurate and authoritative information with regard to the subject matter covered. It is sold with the understanding that the publisher is not engaged in rendering legal, accounting, or other professional advice. If legal advice or other expert assistance is required, the services of a qualified professional person should be sought.
— From a *Declaration of Principles* jointly adopted by a Committee of the American Bar Association and a Committee of Publishers and Associations.

Space constraints prevent us from listing on this page all copyright and credit information for lyrics used by permission in this book. This information appears on page 191.

This book is available at quantity discounts for bulk purchases.
For information, call 1-800-872-5627.

To my friend Mike Fleiss, who's on his way to the top of the charts.
— *Bruce Nash*

To Greg and Renee Arnold, may they always sing in harmony.
— *Allan Zullo*

Contents

Acknowledgments

We wish to thank Brian Carroll, whose knowledge of the music world proved indispensable in compiling this book.

We also appreciate the assistance of Ronny Schiff of Ronny Schiff Productions, Howard and Sandy Benjamin of the Interview Factory, and David Kelly of the Library of Congress.

Among the sources that proved helpful in filling out our stories are *The Billboard Book of Number One Hits* by Fred Bronson, *The Billboard Book of One-Hit Wonders* by Wayne Jancik, *Behind the Hits* by Bob Shannon and John Javna, *Rock Movers and Shakers* by Dafydd Rees and Luke Crampton, *The Top 10* by Bob Gilbert and Gary Theroux, and Joel Whitburn's *Top Pop*.

Answers to rear cover quiz:

#1. *TRUE.* Dees was a popular Memphis disc jockey whose station, WMPS, was faced with an interesting professional dilemma when his song "Disco Duck" started racing up the charts in 1976. If they played the song, would they be leaving themselves open to charges of favoritism? The station resolved the dilemma by firing Dees. See page 173 for all the gory details. Quack.

#2. *FALSE.* Did you get taken in on this one? You were probably thinking of the lyrics to "Louie, Louie," which, though entirely innocent, did cause a minor stir in the sixties because of a host of obscenities its listeners imagined hearing. The governor of Indiana actually moved to have the song banned. (He didn't have any problem with "Bohemian Rhapsody.") The horrible truth about "Louie, Louie," though, is not that its lyrics are obscene; it's that they're *incomprehensible*. If you've always wondered what the hell the song was about, turn to page 93 for the complete lyrics.

#3. *TRUE.* Yep. Strange but true. When John Paul II was rushed to the hospital after the attempt on his life in 1981, Dolce was drafted to fill the empty slot at an outdoor festival at which the pontiff had been scheduled to appear. For more about the immortal "Shaddap You Face," see page 137.

#4. *TRUE.* Talk about strange bedfellows. That's Rizzuto doing the play-by-play on the Tubby One's "Paradise by the Dashboard Light." The full story appears on page 33.

#5. *TRUE.* Anka didn't do much to salvage the situation when he responded to his critics by saying, "I got the kind of flak I expected. We tested it on some chicks first and got all kinds of objections." Want to hear more? See page 161.

The Wacky Top 40

What is it about certain pop songs that make them so . . . wacky? You know the ones. Outrageous, unforgettable—and laughable.

Some tunes are meant to be funny. However, we've all heard songs that weren't intended to make us laugh, but do anyway. They're the really wacky ones.

They assault us with nonsensical lyrics like "Someone left the cake out in the rain . . ." or "Ooo-eee, oo ah-ah, ting-tang, walla-walla, bing-bang."

They drive us batty with bizarre story lines like the dog fancier who was dragged off to the mental ward or the miners who survived a cave-in by eating their buddy.

Sometimes they stir up unintended controversy: "(You're) Having My Baby," made feminists see red, and "Short People" spurred diminutive pop fans to stand tall in outrage.

They even order us to "shaddup you face," "tie me kangaroo, down, sport," and "eat it!"

And they have inspired us to conjure up our playlist of the silliest, funniest, and most laughable songs from the late fifties through the eighties—in *The Wacky Top 40*.

If you don't see your favorite wacky song in this book, write to *The Wacky Top 40*, P.O. Box 31867, Palm Beach Gardens, FL 33420. Maybe we'll include it in a second collection of zany tunes.

Now, on to the show.

TIE A YELLOW RIBBON ROUND THE OLE OAK TREE

Dawn

#40

FOR THE RECORD

Released by Bell Records in 1973.
Playing time: 3:19.
Soared to #1 on the *Billboard* Hot 100 and stayed there for four weeks.
Sold more than 7 million copies.
Was the most popular song of 1973.

BACKGROUND MUSIC

The first time Tony Orlando heard this sentimental song, he refused to record it, thinking it was too sappy. Instead, he tried to convince several other artists to do the record, but could find no takers.

Eventually, Orlando's aversion to the song faded and he and the group Dawn recorded it—and wound up with a mammoth hit that millions loved to hate.

In the early sixties, Orlando—born Michael Anthony Orlando Cassevitis in New York—was a teenage sensation with two Top 40 records, "Halfway to Paradise" and "Bless You." But by 1964, at the age of 20, Orlando's days as a hitmaker seemed to be over.

He remained in the music business as a publishing executive. Then fate stepped in and launched him on another singing career.

One day, two out-of-work producers—Hank Medress and Dave Appell—came to Orlando with a demo called "Candida."

It was performed by a group called Dawn, which included a male lead and two session singers, Telma Hopkins and Joyce Vincent Wilson. Bell Records liked the song but wanted a different male lead.

"Hank and Dave asked me to sing the lead," Orlando recalled. "I told them I couldn't because I worked for CBS and it would be a conflict of interest. I told them, 'I'm not about to lose my job. Forget it, guys.' They said, 'We don't have any money. We're broke. Please help us.' So I said, 'Okay, under one condition. If you sell the record, you can't use my name.' The record got cut under the name

Dawn and it went to number one."

Orlando fessed up to his boss, Clive Davis, about his role in the record. Fortunately, Davis agreed to let him record an album under the name Dawn because, said Orlando, "I told him, 'There's no way there's going to be any more hits with this group.'

"Now Hank and Dave come in with a song called 'Knock Three Times,' and I said, 'Guaranteed this ain't going nowhere. Who's going to buy a record about a guy knocking on a ceiling three times and twice on a pipe?'" To his amazement, the song—released under the name of Dawn—became an even bigger hit than "Candida."

"At that point, it was time to quit my job," said Orlando. "I thought I'd devote my time and money to Dawn."

Meanwhile, songwriters Irwin Levine and L. Russell Brown were inspired to pen a song about a touching true story they had read in the newspaper:

A man who had just been released from prison after serving a three-year sentence for writing bad checks was heading home to White Oak, Georgia, on a bus. A few days earlier, he had written a letter to his wife saying he would understand if she didn't want to see him. But if she still wanted him, she could let him know by tying a yellow ribbon around the

only oak tree in the town square. As the bus rolled in to White Oak, the driver slowed down so all could see what his wife had decided. There, wrapped around the old oak tree, was a yellow ribbon.

"The first time that I listened to the demo, I said, 'This is the corniest song I've ever heard in my life,'" recalled Orlando. "I told [producers] Hank and Dave, 'No way am I singing this song.'

"I tried to pawn off the song on some of my friends. I called Jimmy Darren and said, 'Listen, I've got this great song for you. This is a smash. You had "Goodbye Cruel World." This is perfect for you.' But he turned it down.

"So I sent it to Bobby Vinton and said, 'This is perfect for you. This is a smash.' But he passed, too.

"Three or four months went by and I couldn't find anyone who wanted to record it. But I couldn't stop singing the chorus to 'Tie a Yellow Ribbon.' By now, Dawn and I were working on a new album, 'Tuneweaving,' and I realized this song wouldn't let go of me.

"So I told Hank and Dave, 'Okay, let's go in and give this one a shot.' And that record came off in one take."

"Tie a Yellow Ribbon" became a huge hit and the signature record for Dawn.

NOTEWORTHY NOTES

■ Prior to recording "Tie a Yellow Ribbon," Orlando had never recorded in the same studio with

Dawn singers Telma Hopkins and Joyce Vincent Wilson! Previously, the women had recorded the backing vocals in California, with Orlando adding his part in New York.

- Hopkins and Wilson called themselves Dawn because it was the name of the daughter of their record promotions man, Steve Wax.

— PLATTER PATTER —

Tony Orlando and Dawn were about to split up in 1972 because they were going broke. The surprising success of "Tie a Yellow Ribbon" saved their act.

"Even though we had a couple of hit records, I was putting every dime I made back into the group," said Orlando. "I was about $750,000 in debt because we had a problem with bogus groups."

Because the trio was strictly a studio group at first and didn't tour, no one knew what the members of Dawn looked like. As a result, fake Dawns were performing all over the country.

"There were 50 or 60 of these bogus groups," recalled Orlando. "When we started to tour, promoters would tell me, 'What do we need you for? Nobody knows what Dawn looks like.' So we were working at the same low rates as the bogus groups were. We were getting up to $700 a night when we could have been making thousands.

Michael Ochs Archives

"I was putting out a lot of money for arrangements, the girls' dresses, air fare, hotel rooms, and the overhead was killing me." The financial strain was so great that he and the girls agreed to disband after recording a new album and the single "Tie a Yellow Ribbon."

Thanks to the success of that record, the trio—which changed its name from Dawn to Tony Orlando and Dawn—landed a new musical variety TV show of the same name. They remained together for four more years.

FOLLOW UPS AND DOWNS

Among the follow-up records were "Say, Has Anybody Seen My Sweet Gypsy Rose," #3 in 1973; and "He Don't Love You (Like I Love You)," #1 in 1975.

ROCK ON

The group split up in 1977 when Tony Orlando suffered a nervous breakdown. Since his recovery, he has been singing solo and acting on TV.

Telma Hopkins enjoys an acting career. She has co-starred in such sitcoms as "Bosom Buddies," "Gimme a Break," and "Family Matters."

Tie a Yellow Ribbon 'Round the Ole Oak Tree

I'm comin' home, I've done my time.
Now I've got to know what is and isn't mine.
If you received my letter tellin' you I'd soon be free,
Then you'll know just what to do if you still want me,
If you still want me.

Tie a yellow ribbon round the ole oak tree.
It's been three long years, do ya still want me?
If I don't see a ribbon round the ole oak tree,
I'll stay on the bus, forget about us, put the blame on me,
If I don't see a yellow ribbon round the ole oak tree.

Bus driver, please look for me,
'Cause I couldn't bear to see what I might see.
I'm really still in prison and my love she holds the key,
A simple yellow ribbon's what I need to set me free.
I wrote and told her please.

Tie a yellow ribbon round the ole oak tree.
It's been three long years, do ya still want me?
If I don't see a ribbon round the ole oak tree,
I'll stay on the bus, forget about us, put the blame on me,
If I don't see a yellow ribbon round the ole oak tree.

Now the whole damn bus is cheering, and I can't believe I see
A hundred yellow ribbons round the ole oak tree.

AFTERNOON DELIGHT

Starland Vocal Band

━━━━━━━━ FOR THE RECORD ━━━━━━━━

Released by Windsong Records in 1976.
Playing time: 3:12.
Zoomed to #1 on the *Billboard* Hot 100 for two weeks.
Became a gold single.

━━━━━━━━ BACKGROUND MUSIC ━━━━━━━━

This naughty-but-nice song, with its cheerfully risqué title and lyrics, was inspired by a menu in a restaurant.

Bill Danoff, leader of the Starland Vocal Band, was having lunch at an eatery in Washington, D.C., called Clyde's. As Danoff's wife, Taffy, who was also a Starland singer, explained to audiences before the group would sing the song: "It seems Clyde's has a menu called 'Afternoon Delight' with stuff like spiced shrimp and hot Brie with almonds. So Bill ate it—the food, that is—and went home and explained to me about what Afternoon Delight *should* be."

Before their hit single, the Danoffs were active in the Washington music scene in the sixties. Bill was working as a light and sound man at a night spot called the Cellar Door, where he met John Denver, then part of the Chad Mitchell Trio. The two struck up a friendship and Bill started sending Denver some of his songs. One of them was "I'd Rather Be in Colorado," which Denver recorded. Then, with Taffy, Bill wrote one of Denver's biggest hits, "Take Me Home, Country Roads."

Meanwhile, the Danoffs were part of a five-person singing group called Fat City. When it folded, the couple went out on their own and then formed the Starland Vocal Band with pianist-singer Jon Carroll, who had worked with them on their last album, and vocalist Margot Chapman, who used to be a member of Fat City. It wasn't long before the group became one of the first acts to sign with John Denver's new Windsong label.

Then came that fortuitous lunch at Clyde's.

"I had this Cajun-like melody in my head and I didn't know what to do with it," Danoff recalled. "When I saw those menu specials under 'Afternoon Delight,' I knew it would make a great song title. Then I asked myself, 'What could a song about afternoon delight be about?' The answer was obvious. You tell the phrase to someone and they say, 'Oh, a nooner.'

"I enjoyed writing that song. I put food images in the song, too, because the idea for the record originated in a restaurant."

Admitting that listeners had fun trying to figure out all the innuendoes in the song, Danoff said, "I didn't want to write an all-out sex song. I just wanted to write something that was fun and hinted at sex."

As Taffy so sweetly put it, "We're not the cleanest thing going down the pike."

The Starland Vocal Band thought they might have a problem getting airplay because of the song's naughty lyrics. But few stations objected to it—because most of those program directors who were ultra-conservative didn't get the hidden meanings.

"When it first came out, some stations were hesitant to play it," Danoff told the *Los Angeles Times*. "But that hesitancy didn't last long, although there were times when an AM station wouldn't play it but its sister FM station would.

"If the song had been banned, it would have been a real injustice. The lyrics are subtle and sophisticated and not at all raunchy.

"It might have been banned years ago, but not today."

PLATTER PATTER

The group starred in its own summer replacement TV show that featured a comedy regular who went on to bigger and better things—David Letterman.

In the summer of 1977, following the success of "Afternoon Delight," CBS gave the group its own limited series, "The Starland Vocal Band Show." The whimsical variety show featured music as well as comedy sketches.

Some of the skits were performed by Letterman, who was one of the show's writers. It was the first time that Letterman appeared as a regular on a TV show.

Later, group member Jon Carroll admitted to the press that the series was "a major mistake," adding that "it was a bad show and we knew it early on."

FOLLOW UPS AND DOWNS

The Starland Vocal Band failed to follow up "Afternoon Delight" with any major national success. Their only other charted songs were "California Day," #66 in 1976; "Hail! Hail! Rock and Roll!" #71 in 1977; and "Loving You With My Eyes," #71 in 1980.

ROCK ON

Jon Carroll and fellow member Margot Chapman married each other while Bill and Taffy separated.

Although the group disbanded, each member continues to sing and write on a solo basis.

Michael Ochs Arvhives

Afternoon Delight

Gonna find my baby, gonna hold her
    tight
Gonna grab some afternoon delight
My motto's always been when it's
    right, it's right
Why wait until the middle of a cold,
    dark night
When everything's a little clearer in
    the light of day
And we know the night is always
    gonna be her anyway?

Thinking of you's working up my
    appetite
Looking forward to a little afternoon
    delight
Rubbing sticks and stones together
    make the sparks ignite
And the thought of rubbing you is
    getting so exciting.

Sky rockets in flight
Afternoon delight
Afternoon delight
Afternoon delight.

Started out this morning feeling so
    polite
I always thought a fish could not be
    caught who didn't bite
But you got some bait awaiting and I
    think I might
Like nibbling a little afternoon delight.

Sky rockets in flight
Afternoon delight
Afternoon delight
Afternoon delight.

Be waiting for me, baby, when I come
    around
We can make a lot of loving 'fore the
    sun goes down.

Thinking of you's working up my
    appetite
Looking forward to a little afternoon
    delight
Rubbing sticks and stones together
    make the sparks ignite
And the thought of rubbing you is
    getting so exciting.

Sky rockets in flight
Afternoon delight
Afternoon delight
Afternoon delight
Afternoon delight
Afternoon delight.

SHANNON
Henry Gross

FOR THE RECORD

Released by Lifesong Records in 1976.
Playing time: 3:50.
Climbed to #6 on the *Billboard* Hot 100.
Reached gold status with 1.5 million in sales.

BACKGROUND MUSIC

This seemingly plaintive, sentimental song about a lost love was really nothing more than a sorrowful tune about the death of a dog owned by one of the Beach Boys.

It was written and sung by Henry Gross, who often opened for the famed group.

In 1976, a year after he charted his first single, "One More Tomorrow" (it reached #93), Gross paid a visit to Beach Boy Carl Wilson. "Carl told me that he had an Irish setter named Shannon and it was killed by a car," Gross recalled. "I related to it strongly. At the time I had an Irish setter, too. And her name was Shannon. Corny? Sure, but it really touched me. I knew how I'd feel if my Shannon died. So I went home and sat down and wrote 'Shannon.' I kept thinking about my dog and how much I loved her. I mean, I'm a real animal rights person, an animal activist. I love animals and so it was all the more natural for me to write it.

"After I wrote the song, I put it on a cassette and sent it to Carl, hoping the Beach Boys would record it. But they didn't. In fact, I never heard from anyone about it. So I decided to put it on my next record."

The background music on the record evokes the sound of the ocean— all because of a noisy neighbor. "I was living in an apartment in Queens and there was a guy from Colombia living on the floor directly above me," said Gross. "He had these big speakers on the floor and in the afternoons, when he was home, he'd blast his salsa music. It was really great music, but I couldn't write or think because it was so loud. So I bought an environmental sound record called 'The Ultimate Seashore' and played the sounds of the ocean full blast and drowned out the bass coming from upstairs.

"With the ocean sounds in the room, it really put me in the right frame of mind and I was able to write 'Shannon.' I played the song on a nylon string guitar that I used to take to the beach. The music and the lyrics that I first jotted down on paper remained pretty much unchanged when I went to record the song."

The same time Gross recorded "Shannon," he cut an uptempo record called "Springtime Mama" which the Lifesong executives thought was much better than his ode to a dead dog. "People wanted 'Springtime Mama' to be released first," said Gross. "But I didn't want to hear about it. I loved 'Shannon' and I believed in it totally. To me, the melody was the best thing I'd ever written and I wanted to go with it without further ado. A thousand people told me I was crazy for going with that as the first single. I thought that if this record is not a hit, then I'm done."

The song performed well enough to reach gold status—and it was bought by a good many people who didn't realize it was about a dog. "There were people who thought it was a love song," Gross admitted. "And in a way, they're right. It was about the love of a dog. I loved my Shannon. She lived to be $14\frac{1}{2}$ years old before dying a natural death."

NOTEWORTHY NOTES

- Gross wrote the song in only ten minutes.

- The falsetto vocals on "Shannon" were written because Gross was a big fan of Beach Boy Brian Wilson and was influenced by his singing style.

- Producer Terry Cashman wasn't too excited about the song when he first heard Gross sing it in his office. But when Cashman saw Gross perform the song in concert, he bought Gross' contract from A&M Records and produced the record on his own Lifesong label.

PLATTER PATTER

Henry Gross was one of the founding members of the oldies revival group Sha Na Na.

In 1969, Gross was a political science and speech major at Brooklyn College and played in a band called Orogeny (a scientific word for the formation of mountains). While in school, he accepted an invitation from friends at nearby Columbia University to help them form a new fifties band.

Gross sang lead and played guitar as the wildly animated group performed in such major venues as the Fillmore East, the Fillmore West, and at Woodstock. He eventually left Sha Na Na to go solo.

Michael Ochs Archives

SHANNON   27

FOLLOW UPS AND DOWNS

Gross followed up "Shannon" in 1976 with "Springtime Mama," the song that most of his advisors thought should have been released first. It sold less than half the copies that "Shannon" did, reaching only #37 on the charts.

Gross closed out 1976 with his final chart song, "Someday (I Didn't Want To Have To Be The One)" which made it to #87.

ROCK ON

Henry Gross lives in Nashville where he still composes and owns his own record label. "It's called Zelda Records, named after my mom," he said. Parroting a well-known hair replacement commercial, Gross added, "And I'm not only the president, but I'm a client as well."

Gross has toured with the Doobie Brothers, Billy Joel, Aerosmith, REO Speedwagon, the Allman Brothers, the Charlie Daniels Band, and Air Supply. In 1993, he opened for the Beach Boys.

Shannon

Another day is at end
Mama says she's tired again
No one can even begin to tell her
I hardly know what to say
But maybe it's better that way
If papa were here
I'm sure he'd tell her

Shannon is gone
I hope she's drifting out to sea
She always loved to swim away
Maybe she'll find an island
With a shady tree
Just like the one in our backyard

Mama tries hard to pretend
Things will get better again
Somehow she's keeping
It all inside her
But finally the tears fill our eyes
And I know that somewhere tonight
She knows how much
We really miss her

Shannon is gone
I hope she's drifting out to sea
She always loved to swim away
Maybe she'll find an island
With a shady tree
Just like the one in our backyard
Just like the one in our backyard

TIMOTHY
The Buoys

FOR THE RECORD

Released by Scepter Records in 1971.
Playing time: 2:45.
Peaked at #17 on the *Billboard* Hot 100.

BACKGROUND MUSIC

This bizarre song about cannibalism was written solely to get banned!

"I wrote it because I was hoping the controversy would get attention for the Buoys," said Rupert Holmes (see "Escape [The Piña Colada Song]" on page 43).

Holmes was a struggling 20-year-old arranger and songwriter who was good friends with Michael Wright, a junior engineer at Scepter Records in New York. "Michael had the keys to the studio and, on the weekends, we'd make hundreds of records with any musicians we could find," Holmes recalled.

One of the groups was the Buoys, a young band from Wilkes-Barre, Pennsylvania, whose songs Wright wanted to produce. "They had great voices and they were pretty good on their instruments," said Holmes. "They were a year younger than me and they thought that Michael and I knew everything about recording when we knew practically nothing. We were one page ahead of them."

Although the Buoys had signed a contract with Scepter, the label had virtually ignored them. "We talked about how to get attention for the group," said Holmes. "I came to the conclusion that if I could write them a song that would get banned, it would cause some commotion. Michael could then insist that the record would have been a smash if only it hadn't been banned. Then, if Scepter wasn't interested, he could take the group to another label and make a good deal.

"So I deliberately sat down to write a song that would get banned. I wasn't going to write a song about drugs. And in terms of sexual controversy, the market wasn't ready for that. So I thought, 'What the heck can I do? I'm not going to stick in a bunch of four-letter words just so they can bleep them out.' It had to be something most stations would play but others wouldn't."

One day in his apartment, Holmes was strumming his guitar, working on an arrangement of "Sixteen Tons" for pop singer Andy Kim when he caught a glimpse of the TV set that was on in the next room. It was tuned to the cooking show "The Galloping Gourmet" with Graham Kerr.

"I'm singing a verse from 'Sixteen Tons': 'Some people say that a man is made out of mud/A coal man is made out of muscle and blood/Muscle and blood and skin and bones.' And I think, 'Sounds like a recipe,' because in the next room, the Galloping Gourmet is saying 'Take these chickens, separate the breasts from the wings.' And I think, 'Muscle and blood, skin and bones, bake in a moderate oven for three hours and serve.' I'm thinking mining and I'm thinking food. And then I say, 'Oh, wow! Cannibalism during a mine disaster! That's it!'

"So I spun this tale about three guys trapped in a mine cave-in. But when they're pulled free, there are only two of them left. The narrator of the song can't remember what happened to the third guy, Timothy, and he keeps asking, 'God, why don't I know?' All he knows is he's not hungry anymore."

With Bill Kelly singing the lead, the Buoys recorded "Timothy." As Holmes had hoped, the song generated a wave of controversy. Said the songwriter, "A station would play it and after a few listenings, kids would catch on to what the song was about. Then someone would tell the radio station and the song would be pulled. And the kids would say, 'Why aren't you playing "Timothy"?' And the station would say, 'Because it's not appropriate for you to hear.'

"I knew it was controversial, but banning it *was* ridiculous. I mean, the song wasn't going to cause people to think cannibalism was a good idea."

"Timothy" began a steady climb up the charts; most stations, it turned out, were playing the song. "It would have done better on the charts but some of the big stations in New York and Los Angeles kept it off their playlists," said Holmes.

"College kids loved the song. They even had gatherings called 'The Timothy for Lunch Bunch.'"

NOTEWORTHY NOTES

- The song was written in one draft. "I don't believe I changed one word," said Holmes.
- The E string of lead singer Bill Kelly's guitar kept loosening during the recording session. "We did the whole recording with me holding the tuning peg on his guitar as he strummed and every time it started to slip, I turned the tuning peg back," said Holmes.

Ronald Naschak

PLATTER PATTER

Although Scepter released the single, the company actually had no idea "Timothy" was climbing up the charts. When record executives finally realized the nature of the unexpected and controversial hit, they lied about its cannibalistic theme.

"At the time, Scepter was trying to push a single by one of their artists, Beverly Bremers, who was a straight pop singer," Holmes recalled. "The Scepter promotion men kept complaining they couldn't get the record added to the playlist of some stations because the only thing new added was some record called 'Timothy.' The promo men didn't even know 'Timothy' was on their label."

Only when the record reached the Top 40 did the company bigwigs discover they had a winner. But rather than take advantage of the song's controversy, they tried to whitewash it.

"They copped out on the cannibalism," said Holmes. "They started a rumor that 'Timothy' was a mule, so it wasn't so bad that the survivors ate him. I was offended at the idea of this poor defenseless mule being eaten.

"And still to this day there are people who ask me, 'Now you gotta tell me. Was Timothy a mule?' I say, 'No, Timothy was a man—and they ate him!'"

FOLLOW UPS AND DOWNS

The Buoys followed up "Timothy" with another tall tale about death written by Holmes called "Give Up Your Guns." The song—about a western showdown—barely made it on the charts, rising only to #84.

Incredibly, it soared to #1 in Holland—ten years later! "It had been used in a tire commercial there and the Buoys' original recording caught on with the kids," said Holmes.

ROCK ON

The Buoys still play from time to time in the Wilkes-Barre area. Two original members, Bill Kelly and Joe Jerry, formed a new group called Dakota which plays rock with a tinge of folk and country.

Timothy

*Trapped in a mine that had caved in
And everyone knows the only ones left
Were Joe and me and Tim
When they broke through to pull us
free
The only ones left to tell the tale
Was Joe and me*

*Timothy, Timothy, where on earth did
you go
Timothy, Timothy, God, why don't I
know*

*Hungry as hell, no food to eat
And Joe said that he would sell his
soul
For just a piece of meat
Water enough to drink for two
And Joe said to me, I'll take a swig
And then there's some for you*

*Timothy, Timothy, Joe was looking at
you
Timothy, Timothy, God, what did we do*

*I must have blacked out just 'round
then
'Cause the very next thing I could see
Was the light of the day again
My stomach was full as it could be
And nobody ever got around to
finding Timothy*

*Timothy, Timothy, where on earth did
you go
Timothy, Timothy, God, why don't I
know*

PARADISE BY THE DASHBOARD LIGHT
Meat Loaf

#36

FOR THE RECORD

Released by Cleveland International/Epic Records in 1978.
Playing time: 7:55.
Reached #39 on the *Billboard* Hot 100.
Was re-released in 1993 after it was used in the Steve Martin movie, *Leap of Faith*, but failed to chart.

BACKGROUND MUSIC

This graphic song of a horny teenage boy trying to score with his date in the front seat of his car was written and sung as a mini-rock opera about adolescent sex. While parents who took the time to listen to the lyrics were shocked, kids made it their anthem.

"People either love us or hate us," said composer Jim Steinman, who, with booming 6-foot, 260-pound singer Meat Loaf, may make up rock 'n' roll's oddest odd couple. "I happen to like any strong reaction, so I never minded the criticism. This song is passionate, but I think it's also fun. That's what I love about opera. It's both heroic and silly; deadly serious and absurd."

As Meat Loaf so eloquently put it, "All I can say is, you can't take this shit seriously."

Born in Dallas to a religious family—his mother and aunts sang hymns on Bing Crosby's old radio show—Meat Loaf (whose real name is Marvin Lee Aday) had a rather unhappy childhood. Kids poked fun at him because he was overweight. In seventh grade he stood only 5 feet, 2 inches tall, yet weighed 240 pounds. Having grown taller and even heavier in high school, he joined the choir to get out of study hall, and he tried out for the football team. He was given the nickname Meat Loaf (now his legal name) after he accidentally stepped on his coach's foot and squashed it.

After graduation, Meat Loaf moved to Los Angeles where he formed a rock band called Meat Loaf Soul which later became Popcorn Blizzard. The group opened for such acts as The Who, Ted Nugent, and Johnny and Edgar Winter.

In 1969, while applying for a part time job as a parking lot attendant at the Aquarius Theater, Meat Loaf met an actor from the musical "Hair." At the actor's suggestion, Meat Loaf auditioned for a role in the road production and landed a part. This led to other roles, including his most famous of all—as the lobotomized rocker who gets eaten for dinner in the 1975 cult film *The Rocky Horror Picture Show*.

Meanwhile, he had starred in an Off-Broadway musical written by Steinman, an Amherst graduate who once played in a rock band called Clitoris That Thought It Was a Puppy. Although he loved rock, Steinman had been a classical piano whiz kid who developed such a passion for opera that he once listened to Wagner's 18-hour "Ring" without leaving his bed.

The two hit it off from the start. After a stint with "The National Lampoon Road Show," they decided to team up for an over-the-edge album combining rock and theater.

Steinman sat down and penned absurd, graphic songs of teen life like "Paradise" which he described as "sardonic, operatic, desperate, extreme, and really passionate—there's something dangerous to it. It's an anthem to that moment when you feel like you're on the head of a match that's burning."

Recalled Meat Loaf, "We did thousands of voice and piano sessions for the album. We rehearsed for a year before we brought people to the studio. People either loved or hated the music—most of them hated it."

Rocker-producer Todd Rundgren, however, loved it and put up his own money to help polish the album. When they went looking for a record label, Meat Loaf and Steinman were turned down time and again. They had everything going against them, including record execs' belief that at 260 pounds, Meat Loaf was more of a hulk than a hunk and a turn-off to girls.

Finally, Cleveland International, a fledgling production company, stepped in and persuaded Epic to release the album, entitled "Bat Out of Hell." At a convention of the parent company, CBS Records, Meat Loaf performed on stage where he sang "Paradise" with such lust and fury that he nearly mauled Ellen Foley, who did the female vocals on the record. His raucous performance convinced the bigwigs to get behind the album and release "Paradise" as a single.

"Paradise," said Steinman, has proven to be an "anthem to the essence of rock 'n' roll, to a world that despises inaction and loves passion and rebellion."

NOTEWORTHY

- Phil Rizzuto, former New York Yankees shortstop and radio voice of the team, did the baseball play-by-play featured in the middle of "Paradise."

- Ellen Foley later co-starred on the TV sitcom "Night Court" in 1984-85 as Billie Young.

- The instrumental track was an all-star collaboration featuring members of Todd Rundgren's Utopia, Bruce Springsteen's E Street Band, Edgar Winter, and Jim Steinman.

Michael Ochs Archives

PLATTER PATTER

Meat Loaf would often get so carried away while performing in his live concerts—especially when he sang "Paradise"—that he would stumble, gasping, into the wings for a snort of oxygen straight from the tank.

"There have been times I didn't even remember going out or coming off," he recalled. "I passed out completely in Atlanta. I was paralyzed on the floor. When I came to, I looked up and this gorgeous blonde Scandinavian nurse all in white was leaning over me, asking if I was all right. Shit, I thought I had died and gone to heaven."

In Toronto, while pawing his female backup singer during "Paradise," Meat Loaf was so possessed by the song that he tumbled over the edge of the stage and tore the ligaments in his leg. He ended up in a wheelchair; the tour was postponed for over a month. "I get so possessed by the songs," he said, "and so wrapped up in the show that it's like a withdrawal when it's over."

FOLLOW UPS AND DOWNS

Meat Loaf charted two other songs after "Paradise"—"You Took the Words Right Out of My Mouth," #39 in 1979, and "I'm Gonna Love Her for Both of Us," #84 in 1981.

"Paradise" helped vault the album "Bat Out of Hell" to worldwide sales of over 7 million copies.

ROCK ON

Meat Loaf continues to perform in concert and is especially popular in England and other parts of Europe.

He and Jim Steinman completed a new album called "Bat Out of Hell II" which was released in 1993.

Paradise by the Dashboard Light

BOY:
Well, I remember every little thing
As if it happened only yesterday
Parking by the lake
And there was not another car in sight
And I never had a girl
Looking any better than you did
And all the kids at school
They were wishing they were me that night

And now our bodies are oh so close and
tight
It never felt so good, it never felt so right
And we're glowing like the metal on the
edge of a knife
Glowing like the metal on the edge of a
knife
C'mon! Hold on tight!
Well, c'mon! Hold on tight!

Though it's cold and lonely in the deep
dark night
I can see paradise by the dashboard light

GIRL:
Ain't no doubt about it
We were doubly blessed
Cause we were barely seventeen
And we were barely dressed

Ain't no doubt about it
Baby got to go out and shout it
Ain't no doubt about it
We were doubly blessed

BOY:
Cause we were barely seventeen
And we were barely dressed

Baby doncha hear my heart
You got it drowning out the radio
I've been waiting so long
For you to come along and have some fun

Well, I gotta let you know
No, you're never gonna regret it
So open up your eyes, I got a big surprise
It'll feel all right
Well, I wanna make your motor run

And now our bodies are oh so close and
tight
It never felt so good, it never felt so right
And we're glowing like the metal on the
edge of a knife
Glowing like the metal on the edge of a
knife
C'mon! Hold on tight!
Well, c'mon! Hold on tight!

Though it's cold and lonely in the deep
dark night
I can see paradise by the dashboard light
Though it's cold and lonely in the deep
dark night
Paradise by the dashboard light

You got to do what you can
And let Mother Nature do the rest
Well, ain't no doubt about it
We were doubly blessed
Cause we were barely seventeen
And we were barely . . .

We're gonna go all the way tonight
We're gonna go all the way
And tonight's the night
We're gonna go all the way tonight
We're gonna go all the way
And tonight's the night
We're gonna go all the way tonight
We're gonna go all the way
And tonight's the night
We're gonna go all the way tonight
We're gonna go all the way
And tonight's the night
We're gonna go all the way tonight

We're gonna go all the way
And tonight's the night

RADIO BROADCAST:
OK, here we go, we got a real pressure
  cooker
going here, two down, nobody on, no
  score,
bottom of the ninth, there's the wind-up,
  and
there it is, a line shot up the middle, look
at him go. This boy can really fly!
He's rounding first and really turning it on
now, he's not letting up at all, he's gonna
try for second; the ball is bobbled out in
  center,
and here comes the throw, and what a
  throw!
He's gonna slide in head first, here he
  comes, he's out!
No, wait, safe—safe at second base, this
  kid really
makes things happen out there.
Batter steps up to the plate, here's the
  pitch—
he's going, and what a jump he's got,
  he's trying
for third, here's the throw, it's in the dirt—
safe at third! Holy cow, stolen base!
He's taking a pretty big lead out there,
  almost
daring him to try and pick him off. The
  pitcher
glances over, winds up, and it's bunted,
  bunted
down the third base line, the suicide
  squeeze is on!
Here he comes, squeeze play, it's gonna
  be close,
here's the throw, here's the play at the
  plate,
holy cow, I think he's gonna make it!

GIRL:
Stop right there!
I gotta know right now!
Before we go any further:

Do you love me?
Will you love me forever?
Do you need me?
Will you never leave me?
Will you make me so happy for the rest
  of my life?
Will you take me away and will you
  make me your wife?
Do you love me?
Will you love me forever?
Do you need me?
Will you never leave me?
Will you make me so happy for the rest
  of my life?
Will you take me away and will you
  make me your wife?
I gotta know right now
Before we go any further
Do you love me?
Will you love me forever?

BOY:
Well, let me sleep on it
Baby, baby let me sleep on it
Well, let me sleep on it
I'll give you an answer in the morning

Well, let me sleep on it
Baby, baby let me sleep on it
Well, let me sleep on it
I'll give you an answer in the morning

Well, let me sleep on it
Baby, baby let me sleep on it
Well, let me sleep on it
I'll give you an answer in the morning

GIRL:
I gotta know right now!
Do you love me?
Will you love me forever?
Do you need me?
Will you never leave me?
Will you make me so happy for the rest
  of my life?
Will you take me away and will you

PARADISE BY THE DASHBOARD LIGHT   37

make me your wife?
I gotta know right now
Before we go any further
Do you love me?
Will you love me forever?

What's it gonna be, boy?
C'mon, I can't wait all night
What's it gonna be, boy?
Yes or no?
What's it gonna be, boy?
Yes or no?

BOY:
Well, let me sleep on it
Baby, baby let me sleep on it
Well, let me sleep on it
I'll give you an answer in the morning
Let me sleep on it

GIRL:
Will you love me forever?

BOY:
Well, let me sleep on it

GIRL:
Will you love me forever?

BOY:
I couldn't take it any longer
Lord I was crazed

And when the feeling came upon me
Like a tidal wave
I started swearing to my god and on my
*   mother's grave*
That I would love you to the end of time
I swore I would love you to the end of
*   time*

So now I'm praying for the end of time
To hurry up and arrive
Cause if I gotta spend another minute
*   with you*
I don't think that I can really survive
I'll never break my promise or forget my
*   vow*
But God only knows what I can do right
*   now*
I'm praying for the end of time
It's all that I can do
Praying for the end of time, so I can end
*   my time with you*

BOY:
It was long ago and it was far away
And it was so much better than it is today

GIRL:
It never felt so good
It never felt so right
And we were glowing like
A metal on the edge of a knife

MORE, MORE, MORE
Andrea True Connection

FOR THE RECORD

Released by Buddah Records in 1976.
Playing time: 3:02.
Rose to #4 on the *Billboard* Hot 100, becoming a gold record.

BACKGROUND MUSIC

This explicit orgasmic disco ditty became the only Top 10 hit ever posted by a porno film queen.

Before the record was released, Nashville-born Andrea True had starred in such X-rated skin flicks as *Every Inch a Lady*, *Deep Throat II*, and *The Seduction of Lynn Carter*. But she always wanted to be a singer. An itinerant drummer and a wealthy gynecologist helped make her dream come true.

Gregg Diamond was a 22-year-old drummer who had played in clubs and studios for such big names as James Brown, Sonny & Cher, the Guess Who, Melanie, and Joey Dee and the Starliters. In 1973, he decided to go out on his own as a songwriter. "Months went by and I ran out of money and lost my apartment," he recalled. "But rather than go back to playing studio drums, I was determined to get into the music business as a producer, writer, and instrumentalist."

Diamond moved his piano into an empty room of an office building where he composed at night and worked for weeks and weeks on an untitled song.

"It had energy and it reeked of sex," said Diamond. "All I knew was I just had to keep working on this song." Although it had no title or lyrics, he cut a demo of the song with the help of friends.

Then suddenly, out of the blue, Andrea True called him from Jamaica where she was living with her boyfriend. "She said she had heard of me from a mutual friend," Diamond recalled. "When I admitted I wasn't aware of who she was, she said, 'Well, I'm highly insulted.' Then she told me, 'I hear you have something on tape that's really good and I want to sing it and break into the record business. I'll pay for your plane ticket to Jamaica, your room and board, and the studio time.'"

The next day, Diamond flew to Kingston with his drums, keyboards, and tape of the song. "Andrea met me in this low-cut dress," recalled Diamond. "She took me over to her limo where she introduced me to her boyfriend, a gynecologist. He reached out his hand and said, 'I hope you do good.' Then we drove to his place. It was like a palace and he gave me my own house with a pool to use."

The doctor had bought studio time at Federal Records in Kingston for Diamond to produce the record. After a couple of days of laying down tracks for the instrumentals, Diamond still hadn't come up with any lyrics for Andrea to sing. "The doctor came in to the studio on the third day and asked, 'Do you really have a song here?' And I said, 'Of course. Just give me 48 hours.'"

Diamond went down to the beach where he came up with the song's first three words: "More, more, more." To celebrate, he took a cab to the other side of the island where he had a few drinks at a club called Rick's Cafe. Then, on the way back to Kingston, he started writing the lyrics.

"And it just came as sexy as I imagined it," he said. "I had one of those tiny tape recorders and as I played it back, it sounded so excellent, so powerful: 'So take me where you want to/ May my heart you steal/ More, more, more/ How do you like

it?/ How do you like it?' The cab driver loved it and said, 'Oh, man, with that music, it's a free ride.'

"I still didn't have all the lyrics. All I had were the hook and verses. About two in the morning, I woke up Andrea True and said, 'You're gonna sing this.' And I wrote the lyrics of what I had so far on a legal pad.

"So I put the tape on and it came to my attention that she couldn't sing! Then I thought, 'I'm never gonna get off this island. I am totally screwed.' But I went ahead and taught her the song until daybreak. Then, on the way to the studio that morning, I wrote the rest of the words."

After 72 hours of recording, mixing, remixing, and electronically enhancing True's voice, Diamond had finished the song. He returned to New York where he played the record for Art Kass at Buddah Records. The two took the record to one of the Big Apple's hottest disco clubs, which previewed new songs. "The guy put it on, and everybody got up and danced," said Diamond. "It was like lemmings to the sea. Immediately, I got a contract for world rights."

━━━ NOTEWORTHY NOTES ━━━

The only way Gregg Diamond could get Andrea True to relax and sound sexy on the song was to make her feel as though she were on the set of a porno movie.

"I wanted to hear sex through the mike," said Diamond.

"I told her, 'Make it feel like a porno set. Pull your blouse down a little. Take your panties off. Take your shoes off. Now give me your best, sexy breathing . . . give me a long *ooooh*.'"

— PLATTER PATTER —

Although she's credited with singing her songs on the follow-up album, Andrea True never sang them. So claims Gregg Diamond, who produced the LP.

"She didn't cut one lick; she couldn't sing even one note," Diamond revealed. "So you know what I did? I created her vocally. I manufactured the whole album with two background singers.

"I sent a voice print of Andrea to Ohio State University and got the exact amplitude. I got the whole chart on her vocally; the range, everything. The girls then duplicated her voice. Everything on that album sounds more like Andrea than even she does."

When asked if Andrea knew what he had done, Diamond replied, "Of course."

———— FOLLOW UPS AND DOWNS ————

After her debut hit, Andrea True "recorded" the following charted songs: "Party Line," #80, in 1976; "N.Y., You Got Me Dancing," #27 in 1977; and "What's Your Name, What's Your Number?" #56 in 1978.

———————— ROCK ON ————————

Gregg Diamond became one of the most influential disco writer-producers of the 1970s with his own group Bionic Boogie. He worked with artists like Luther Vandross and Whitney Houston before they became famous. Today, Diamond still writes and produces.

Meanwhile, Andrea dropped out of the music (and porno) scene and hasn't been heard from since.

More, More, More

Ooh, how do you like your love?
Ooh, how do you like your love?

But if you want to know
How I really feel
Get the cameras rolling
Get the action going

Baby you know
My love for you is real
Take me where you want to
May my heart you steal

More, more, more
How do you like it?
How do you like it?
More, more, more
How do you like it?
How do you like it?
More, more, more
How do you like it?
How do you like it?

Ooh, how do you like your love?
Ooh, how do you like your love?

But if you want to know
How I really feel
Just get the cameras rolling
Get the action going

Baby you know
My love for you is real
So take me where you want to
May my heart you steal

More, more, more
How do you like it?
How do you like it?
More, more, more
How do you like it?
How do you like it?
More, more, more
How do you like it?
How do you like it?

But if you want to know
How I really feel
Get the cameras rolling
Get the action going

More, more, more
How do you like it?
How do you like it?
More, more, more
How do you like it?
How do you like it?
More, more, more
How do you like it?
How do you like it?

ESCAPE
(THE PIÑA COLADA SONG)

Rupert Holmes

FOR THE RECORD

Released by Infinity Records in 1979.
Playing time: 3:50.
Soared to #1 on the *Billboard* Hot 100, where it remained for two weeks.
Sold over 1.5 million copies.

BACKGROUND MUSIC

Rupert Holmes was reading the classifieds in the *Village Voice* one day when he was struck with the idea of writing a song about a bored lover who unwittingly answers his girlfriend's personal ad.

"The song was spun out of the reality of New York in the late seventies," said Holmes, who back then was well-known in the music world but not to the general public.

After dropping out of the Manhattan School of Music, Holmes arranged songs for the Drifters and Platters and scored everything from TV commercials to porno flicks.

Holmes lived at the Continental Hyatt House in Hollywood, where things apparently got pretty hectic for a while. "I learned everything I know about sex in the elevator," he claimed. "The Rolling Stones had the entire floor above mine. If the groupies couldn't get to Mick, the guy in the room below was okay. I got the rejects."

During the era of bubblegum music, Holmes was one of many anonymous writers who cranked out songs under fictitious group names. He turned out dozens of songs without credit. "I've had hit records I've yet to see a penny from, but the bubblegum factories let me learn my craft," he said.

Eventually, Holmes wrote and recorded more meaningful songs about relationships. "I'm the stunt man of romance," he once said. "I've been falling in love since I was three." But his own records failed to excite the public.

While his singing career languished, Holmes kept afloat writing songs recorded by Barry Manilow, Dolly Parton, and Mac Davis. In 1975, he arranged and co-produced Barbra

Streisand's LP "Lazy Afternoon."

Then one day in 1979, Holmes was reading the personals in the *Village Voice*. "I always found them very amusing because people would describe themselves so glowingly that I thought, 'If they're this person, why on earth would they need to advertise in a newspaper?'" said Holmes. "Then I thought, 'Maybe someone just wants to meet another person and experience the drama and fun of going into a bar and seeing who this person is who responded to your ad.'

"I knew what would happen if I tried that. I would go into the bar and find the person who answered my ad was the woman I was already involved with. That's when I started writing 'Escape.'

"I made the narrator vain. He says he's tired of his lady, yet she's the one who placed the ad. He's not sensitive enough to pick up that she's tired of him. And then I tried to think of a way to make this a happy resolution. I came up with the idea, 'Gee, I was looking for this escape and you were looking for it, so maybe we have more in common than we've allowed ourselves the chance to find out.'"

The lyrics came long after Holmes had written the music. "I had this riff that I was attracted to that had kind of a Latin calypso feel," he said. "I wrote several different lyrics to the music, but none of them seemed to fit. One started out, 'That's the law of the jungle in the school of the street/You get out of the kitchen if you can't take the heat.' I rejected it because it sounded like Billy Joel."

NOTEWORTHY NOTES

- Because it reached the top of the charts in December of 1979 and remained until January of 1980, "Escape" was the last #1 record of the seventies and the first #1 record of the eighties. "I tell people I had the #1 record in two decades without interruption," said Holmes.

- Like many of the songs in this book, "Escape" was a hit that surprised its creator. "I didn't have a sense when I recorded it that the song was going to be a number one hit," said Holmes.

- Holmes' label, Infinity, folded just as "Escape" started climbing up the charts.

- One of the drummers on "Escape" fell asleep during the recording session.

- When Holmes appeared on "The Merv Griffin Show," the producers ordered him to put on an Hawaiian shirt and sing the song while making a piña colada in a blender. He sang without making the drink.

PLATTER PATTER

The original lyrics contained no mention of piña coladas. At the last moment, during the recording session, Rupert Holmes added a lyric mentioning the tropical drink.

"The song had nothing to do with piña coladas," said Rupert Holmes. "I had originally written the line to go, 'If you like Humphrey Bogart and getting caught in the rain.' I put the lyrics up on a music stand and started to sing it. And as I got to the chorus, I was thinking that the line didn't sound right.

"'This is a song about a fellow looking for a fantasy, looking for an escape,' I thought. 'Fantasy Island, drinking from a hollowed-out pineapple with flags of all the nations sticking out of it. I need a tropical drink. Mai Tai? Daiquiri? Piña colada? That's it!'

"I hated the drink because it's too sweet. I drank bourbon. But the word piña colada rolled out of my mouth. So while I was recording the song, every time I came to the line that mentioned Humphrey Bogart, I substituted it with the words 'piña coladas.'"

The song was released as "Escape." But when it started climbing up the charts, the record company, Infinity, wanted to make a change in the title. Too many people were going into the stores asking, "Do you have that

Michael Ochs Archives

piña colada record?" So the record execs decided to lengthen the title by adding, in parentheses, "The Piña Colada Song."

Said Holmes, "I was really against that. But my label said, 'If we don't do it, it's not going to sell as many copies.' So I said, 'Hey, "The Piña Colada Song" sounds good to me.'

"I regret to this day that I didn't cut some deal with a company that makes piña colada mix. And if only I had a royalty for every person who took out a personal ad that said, 'If you like piña coladas . . .'"

FOLLOW UPS AND DOWNS

Holmes followed up his chart-topper with "Him" which peaked at #6 in 1980 and "Answering Machine," #32, later that same year.

ROCK ON

Holmes is still composing, singing, arranging, and producing. He's also written the books for three Broadway plays, including the critically acclaimed "The Mystery of Edwin Drood."

Escape (The Piña Colada Song)

I was tired of my lady
We'd been together too long
Like a worn-out recording
Of a favorite song.
So while she lay there sleeping
I read the paper in bed
And in the personal columns
There was this letter I read:

"If you like Piña Coladas
And getting caught in the rain,
If you're not into yoga
If you have half a brain
If you'd like making love at midnight
In the dunes on the Cape,
Then I'm the love that you've looked
*   for:*
Write to me and escape."

I didn't think about my lady
I know that sounds kind of mean
But me and my old lady
Have fallen into the same old dull
*   routine.*
So I wrote to the paper
Took out a personal ad
And though I'm nobody's poet
I thought it wasn't half-bad:

"Yes I like Piña Coladas
And getting caught in the rain,
I'm not much into health food,
I am into champagne.
I've got to meet you by tomorrow noon
And cut through all this red tape
At a bar called O'Malley's
Where we'll plan our escape."

So I waited with high hopes
And she walked in the place
I knew her smile in an instant
I knew the curve of her face
It was my own lovely lady
And she said, "Oh it's you"
Then we laughed for a moment
And I said, "I never knew

That you liked Piña Coladas
And getting caught in the rain
And the feel of the ocean
And the taste of champagne
If you'd like making love at midnight
In the dunes on the Cape
You're the lady I've looked for
Come with me and escape."

WITCH DOCTOR
David Seville (Ross Bagdasarian)

#33

Released by Liberty Records in 1958.
Playing time: 2:15.
Soared to the top of the charts in April, where it remained for three weeks.
Sold 1.5 million copies.

────── BACKGROUND MUSIC ──────

The song with the squeaky-voiced character spouting unintelligible lyrics was written in a last-ditch effort to save a songwriter and a record company from financial ruin.

This zany tune about a witch doctor giving advice to the lovelorn became an instant hit, salvaging Liberty Records and launching creator Ross Bagdasarian into a lucrative career in novelty songs.

The road to success was a long one for Bagdasarian, a songwriter who had followed in his father's footsteps and become a grape grower in his hometown of Fresno, California. "After a full year of frustration, I harvested the grapes, only to find out the bottom had fallen out of the market," he once recalled. "My wife and I ate a lot of grapes that year."

Almost always broke, Bagdasarian, his wife, and two children moved to Los Angeles where he landed some small acting roles and began writing songs. "In late 1957, my family was down to about $200," said his son Ross Jr. "My dad decided to take about $190 of that to buy a new tape recorder."

Determined to come up with a big hit, Ross Sr. tried to create a novelty tune. "My mind was a little madder than its normal semi-orderly state of confusion," he once told reporters. "I looked up from my desk and saw a book, *Duel with the Witch Doctor*. All the teenage records that were selling seemed to have one thing in common—you couldn't understand any of the lyrics. So I decided to have the witch doctor give advice to the lovelorn in his own language—a kind of qualified gibberish."

After first recording the orchestra track, Bagdasarian spent two months trying to think of a voice for the witch doctor. One day, while fooling around with the tape recorder, he sang into the machine while it was running at half-speed and then played it back at full-speed. Suddenly, Bagdasarian realized he had created a high-pitched Munchkin-like voice for the witch doctor that was perfect for the nonsensical lyrics like "Ooo-eee, ooo ah-ah, ting-tang, walla-walla, bing-bang."

Recalled Ross Jr., "I was about eight at the time and I remember my dad asking the kids to come into the back room to listen to the thing. We just loved it. We honestly didn't know whether it was good, bad, or musically well done, but we just loved it. And we thought that it would be popular with other kids."

But Bagdasarian was faced with two big questions. Could he find a record company? And would the song sell? He went to Si Waronker, co-owner of Liberty Records. "Dad was broke and Liberty Records was about to go under because of a back-taxes debt," said Ross Jr. "Had the people at Liberty not been as desperate as they were, they never would have put out 'Witch Doctor.' They thought it was ridiculous, absolute nonsense.

"My dad said, 'Look, you're already close to bankruptcy. You've got nothing to lose.' So they figured they would give it a try. And, of course, it became a huge hit."

NOTEWORTHY NOTES

Ross Bagdasarian took the name David Seville after the executives at Liberty Records felt his Armenian surname was too hard to pronounce. He chose his new last name because he had been stationed in Seville, Spain, while in the Air Force.

PLATTER PATTER

Bagdasarian was the cousin of famed playwright William Saroyan. In fact, Bagdasarian acted in a Broadway production of Saroyan's play "The Time of Your Life."

Later, when Bagdasarian returned to Los Angeles, he wrote a song that he was convinced was good. "I kept singing the song to anyone who would stand still long enough for the first chorus," he once said. "Pretty soon, Columbia Records heard about it and Rosemary Clooney recorded it." The song was "Come On-a My House"—which zoomed all the way to the top of the charts in 1951.

FOLLOW UPS AND DOWNS

"Witch Doctor" inspired a unique sound that made Bagdasarian a fortune. He loved the high-pitched voice so much that he decided to come up with different characters who sounded just as zany. "I thought if one voice with the witch doctor would do well, why not three voices?" Bagdasarian said in 1965. "But I didn't know what form they would take. Butterflies? Ants? Grasshoppers?

"Then one day while driving to Yosemite National Park, I brought my car to a sudden stop when a chipmunk walked out into the middle of the road and just dared me and my car to drive past him." Bagdasarian was so taken by the critter's audacity that he decided to make the characters of his next song three singing chipmunks.

Six months after "Witch Doctor" had reached #1, Bagdasarian's "The Chipmunk Song" (sometimes known as "Christmas Don't Be Late") was released. It became the fastest-moving record in history, selling 4.5 million copies in just seven weeks. (The Beatles came along a few years later and broke Bagdasarian's record.)

PHOTO COURTESY: Michael Ochs Archives

ROCK ON

Bagdasarian went on to develop the Chipmunks into the most successful novelty creation in music history, with over 35 million records sold.

Tragically, Bagdasarian didn't get a chance to enjoy his success fully. He died of a heart attack in 1972 at the age of 50.

The Chipmunk empire, which includes books, videos, records, and 250 licensed products, is now directed by his son Ross Jr.

Witch Doctor

I told the witch doctor
I was in love with you
I told the witch doctor
I was in love with you
And then the witch doctor
He told me what to do.

He said that
Ooo-eee, ooo ah-ah, ting-tang,
  walla-walla, bing bang
Ooo-eee, ooo ah-ah, ting-tang,
  walla-walla, bing bang
Ooo-eee, ooo ah-ah, ting-tang,
  walla-walla, bing bang
Ooo-eee, ooo ah-ah, ting-tang,
  walla-walla, bing bang.

I told the witch doctor
You didn't love me true
I told the witch doctor
You didn't love me nice
And then the witch doctor
He game me this advice.

He said that
Ooo-eee, ooo ah-ah, ting-tang,
  walla-walla, bing bang
Ooo-eee, ooo ah-ah, ting-tang,
  walla-walla, bing bang
Ooo-eee, ooo ah-ah, ting-tang,
  walla-walla, bing bang
Ooo-eee, ooo ah-ah, ting-tang,
  walla-walla, bing bang

You've been keeping love from me
Just like you were a miser
And I'll admit I wasn't very smart
So I went out and found myself
A guy that's so much wiser
And he taught me the way to win your
  heart.

My friend the witch doctor
He taught me what to say
My friend the witch doctor
He taught me what to do
I know that you'll be mine
When I say this to you.

Ooo-eee, ooo ah-ah, ting-tang,
  walla-walla, bing bang
Ooo-eee, ooo ah-ah, ting-tang,
  walla-walla, bing bang
Ooo-eee, ooo ah-ah, ting-tang,
  walla-walla, bing bang
Ooo-eee, ooo ah-ah, ting-tang,
  walla-walla, bing bang

You've been keeping love from me
Just like you were a miser
And I'll admit I wasn't very smart
So I went out and found myself
A guy that's so much wiser
And he taught me the way to win your
  heart.

My friend the witch doctor
He taught me what to say
My friend the witch doctor
He taught me what to do
I know that you'll be mine
When I say this to you.

Oh baby, ooo-eee, ooo ah-ah,
  ting-tang, walla-walla, bing bang
Ooo-eee, ooo ah-ah, ting-tang,
  walla-walla, bing bang
Come on and ooo-eee, ooo ah-ah,
  ting-tang, walla-walla, bing bang
Ooo-eee, ooo ah-ah, ting-tang,
  walla-walla, bing bang

David Seville (Ross Bagdasarian)

WOOLY BULLY

Sam the Sham & the Pharaohs

#32

FOR THE RECORD

Released by MGM Records in 1965.
Playing time: 2:20.
Peaked at #2 on the *Billboard* Hot 100.
Was a gold single, selling over 3 million copies.

BACKGROUND MUSIC

The title and chorus of this nonsensical but catchy song was a last-second improvisation.

Who or what was a "Wooly Bully"?

It was the name of Sam the Sham's cat!

Sam, who's real name is Domingo Samudio, grew up in Dallas where he formed a high school rock band in the late fifties with several of his friends. Among them was Trini Lopez, who later rose to stardom for singing such hits as "If I Had a Hammer" (#3 in 1963) and "Lemon Tree" (#20 in 1965). After graduation, Samudio spent four years in the Navy before attending college in Texas where he taught himself to play the organ.

While going to school, he studied classical music during the day and played in a rock band at night in local clubs. Within two years, he dropped out of college and joined a traveling carnival as a sideshow pitchman. But that didn't last long. His love for music was so strong that he quit the carny life and joined a band called Andy and the Night Riders, which gained steady work playing clubs in Louisiana and Tennessee.

Eventually the band broke up. Samudio formed a new group in 1963 and wanted to give it a clever name. Because he was the leader of the band and most everyone had been calling him Sam—short for Samudio—he thought it needed to have a name like "Sam the something and the somethings."

When Sam sang, he liked to sham—a rhythm and blues term referring to the gyrations of a vocalist who wiggles, dances, twists, and laughs while singing. So he settled on the first half of the group's name—Sam the Sham.

While the other band members were trying to figure out what to call themselves, they all went to see the 1956 epic film *The Ten Commandments*. Since Ramses, the King of Egypt, looked pretty cool to the musicians, they decided to become the Pharaohs.

Decked out in garish, brightly-colored, Arab clothes, Sam the Sham & the Pharaohs began playing lively, upbeat tunes while tossing humor and shamming into their act. They mugged and jived with each other during sets, much to the delight of their growing legion of fans.

After the group cut a couple of records locally, they caught the attention of MGM Records in 1964. For their first record for MGM, Samudio pulled out one of his favorite compositions and headed to the studio with the Pharaohs.

"We said we had something they might dig, a beat that was pretty popular around Dallas," Sam recalled in the book *The Top Ten*. "The words we were using came from 'The Hully Gully.'" The Hully Gully was a dance mentioned in several charted songs, including "(Baby) Hully Gully" by the Olympics (#72 in 1960); "Hully Gully Again" by Little Caesar & the Romans (#54 in 1961); and "Hully Gully Baby" by the Dovells (#25 in 1962).

But moments before the recording session, executives for MGM informed the group they couldn't record a song about the Hully Gully.

"I said, 'O.K., let's kick it off, and I'll make something up,'" Samudio recalled. "Now, the name of my cat was Wooly Bully, so I started from there." He substituted the original words "Hully Gully" with "Wooly Bully" and just kept improvising.

"The countdown part of the song was also not planned," he said. "I was just goofing around and counted off in Tex-Mex ['Uno, dos, one, two, tres, quatro']. It just blew everybody away, and actually, I wanted it taken off the record. I was a little insecure, I guess.

"Anyway, we did three takes, all of them different, and all of them good. They took the first take and released it. From what I understand, it became the first American record to sell a million copies during the onslaught of all the British groups."

PLATTER PATTER

Even though the lyrics to "Wooly Bully" are not at all suggestive, several radio stations actually banned the song.

After the brouhaha over whether the 1963 hit "Louie Louie" was dirty, stations were leery of songs with words that were hard to understand. So some overly cautious and paranoid program directors wrongly suspected that lyrics like "pull the wool with you" were obscene. As a result, a number of uptight local broadcast censors kept "Wooly Bully" off their playlists.

Naturally, the banning only helped spur publicity for the record, which, in turn, translated into more sales. Much to the prudish program directors' chagrin, "Wooly Bully" was nominated for a Grammy Award and was named Record of the Year by *Billboard*.

Michael Ochs Archives

FOLLOW UPS AND DOWNS

Sam the Sham & the Pharaohs followed up their hit with "Ju Ju Hand," #26, and "Ring Dang Doo," #33, in 1965. The next year, they scored with "Lil' Red Riding Hood," #2, (their second gold single) and "The Hair on My Chinny Chin Chin," #22.

ROCK ON

After going on a world tour, the group broke up in 1968 when their popularity as humorous musical entertainers began to wane.

Domingo Samudio, who performed as a solo act before moving into the record promotion business, lives in Nashville, where he still writes songs.

Wooly Bully

Matty told Hatty
About a thing she saw
Had two big horns
And a wooly jaw.

Wooly bully
Wooly bully
Wooly bully
Wooly bully
Wooly bully.

Hatty told Matty
Let's don't take no chance
Let's not be L 7
Come and learn to dance.

Wooly bully
Wooly bully
Wooly bully
Wooly bully
Wooly bully.

Matty told Hatty
That's the thing to do
Get you someone really
To pull the wool with you.

Wooly bully
Wooly bully
Wooly bully
Wooly bully
Wooly bully.

MONSTER MASH

*Bobby "Boris" Pickett
and the Crypt-Kickers*

FOR THE RECORD

Released by Garpax Records in 1962.
Playing time 3:01.
Soared to #1 on the *Billboard* Hot 100 and stayed there for two weeks, becoming
a gold single.
Returned to the charts in 1970, when it reached #91.
Was re-re-released by Parrot Records in 1973, climbing to #10 and selling more
records—2 million—than it did the first time around.

BACKGROUND MUSIC

A childhood fascination with horror movies and Boris Karloff led to this weird graveyard smash.

While Bobby Pickett was growing up in Somerville, Massachusetts, he used to go to all the movies he wanted to because his father was the manager of a local theater. "I would sit there and watch horror films two or three times a day," recalled Pickett. "I was fascinated with the horror genre and I loved Boris Karloff."

Pickett eventually perfected a dead-on imitation of his favorite horror film star. "I would enter these talent contests in local bars and clubs and do this schtick about Boris Karloff," he recalled. "It lasted about four minutes and I'd always win."

In the late 1950s, Pickett, bitten by the acting bug, moved to Holly-wood and landed some bit parts on TV and in film. In 1962, between acting gigs, Pickett sang with friends in a group called the Cordials. They specialized in doo-wop music and performed at local clubs. One of the songs they sang was the Diamonds' 1957 hit "Little Darlin'." It featured a monologue which Pickett did in his Karloff impersonation: "My darlin,' I need you to hold in mine your little hand / I know too soon that all is grand."

Recalled Pickett, "The kids in the audience would crack up. Lenny Capizzi [one of the members of the Cordials] told me, 'That's a great voice for a novelty record.'" But Pickett didn't think much of the idea at the time. He quit the group shortly thereafter because the other members were always late for rehearsals.

"But then my agent died of a heart attack and I thought, 'Gee, my acting career isn't doing so well.' So I called Lenny and said, 'Let's test out that idea you had.'

"We got together and he sat at the piano and started playing four chords—G, E minor, C, and D. I said, 'Okay, let's call it "The Monster Twist." But Lenny said, 'No, the Twist is out and the Mashed Potato is in. It's "The Monster Mashed Potato."

"Then I wrote, 'I was working in the lab late one night and my eyes beheld an eerie sight . . .' And in less than two hours we had the whole thing written."

They took the song to producer Gary Paxton, whom they had met a few months earlier. "When I was with the Cordials, we used to go to Will Rogers State Beach every Sunday afternoon and sing doo-wop a cappella," said Pickett. "Within ten minutes, a hundred people would encircle us and listen to our music. One day, this cute red headed girl walked up and said, 'My old man is Gary Paxton. He sang "Alley Oop" and he produces now. He'd love you guys. Call him.'

"Gary loved our song and decided to call it 'The Mean Monster Mashed Potato.' But after talking it over, we decided that just 'Monster Mash' was fine. Then Gary told me, 'From now on, you're Bobby 'Boris' Pickett.'

"Every major record label that Gary visited turned 'Monster Mash' down. They said it would never get on the radio and that it was stupid. Gary told me, 'Don't worry. This is a number one record and I'm going to put it out on my own label.'

"He pressed 1,000 records on his label, Garpax, put them in the back of his old Excalibur and drove up and down California, dropping off records at every radio station along the way. And by the time he returned to Los Angeles, the song was on its way to becoming a hit."

NOTEWORTHY NOTES

- Although Pickett had never been in a recording studio before, he did the song in one take.

- The musician who had booked time in the studio right before Pickett's session was Herb Alpert, who also was recording his first song that day.

- The sound of the coffin opening was made by pulling a rusty nail out of a 2-by-4 with the claw of a hammer.

- The bubbling sounds came from blowing through a straw in a glass of water.

- The sound of the chains was made by dropping chains onto plywood planks on the studio floor.

The Original
MONSTER MASH

BOBBY (BORIS) PICKETT and The Crypt-Kickers

MONSTER MASH
RABIAN-THE FIENDAGE IDOL
BLOOD BANK BLUES
GRAVEYARD SHIFT
SKULLY GULLY
WOLFBANE
MONSTER MINUET
TRANSYLVANIA TWIST
SINISTER STOMP
ME & MY MUMMY
MONSTER MOTION
MONSTER MASH PARTY
IRRESISTIBLE IGOR
BELLAS' BASH
LET'S FLY AWAY

Bobby (Boris) Pickett

GARPAX

MONO GPX 57001

Michael Ochs Archives

PLATTER PATTER

Elvis Presley thought "Monster Mash" was one of the dumbest songs ever recorded.

"I was a real Elvis fan," said Bobby Pickett. "One day after the song had become a hit, I bumped into this girl who used to hang around Elvis' house in Los Angeles. So I asked her, 'How's the King?'

"'Well, he hates your record, Bobby,' she said. When I asked why, she told me, 'He thinks it's the stupidest thing he's ever heard.'

"So I said, 'Well, whoever liked him anyway?' I don't think he knew who Boris Karloff was, to tell you the truth."

Although Karloff was alive when the record was released, Pickett never met him. "I heard that he was in a record store and was buying my album, which had 'Monster Mash' on it, and a friend of mine was there and said, 'Oh, Mr. Karloff, I know the young man who did the song and he's a real big fan of yours.' And Karloff said, 'I love his record.' So I was thrilled."

FOLLOW UPS AND DOWNS

Bobby Pickett followed up his smash hit with a song that, he says, "I didn't like and I didn't want to do."

It was called "Monster's Holiday" and reached #30. Among other songs that he later recorded were: "Smoke, Smoke, Smoke That Cigarette," "Star Drek" (he was Captain Jerk), "King Kong, Your Song," and "Monster Rap."

ROCK ON

Bobby Pickett, who lives near New York City, still acts in small theater productions, does commercials and performs at a few singing gigs.

"I never thought in a million years that this record would be the national anthem of Halloween, but it is," he said. "Every Halloween I feel like Guy Lombardo because I get these phone calls and the song gets a tremendous amount of exposure. As a friend once said, 'If you never, ever do another thing the rest of your life, you are a man of history.' I'd like to believe that's true."

Monster Mash

I was working in the lab late one night
When my eyes beheld an eerie sight
For my monster from his slab began
to rise
And suddenly to my surprise

He did the mash
He did the monster mash
The monster mash
It was a graveyard smash
He did the mash
It caught on in a flash
He did the mash
He did the monster mash.

From my laboratory in the castle east
To the master bedroom where the
vampires feast
The ghouls all came from their
humble abodes
To get a jolt from my electrodes

They did the mash
They did the monster mash
The monster mash
It was a graveyard smash
They did the mash
It caught on in a flash
They did the mash
They did the monster mash.

The zombies were having fun
The party had just begun
The guests included Wolf Man
Dracula and his son.

The scene was rockin', all were
  digging the sounds
Igor on chains, backed by his baying
  hounds
The coffin-bangers were about to
  arrive
With their vocal group, "The
  Crypt-Kicker Five"

They played the mash
They played the monster mash
The monster mash
It was a graveyard smash
They played the mash
It caught on in a flash
They played the mash
They played the monster mash.

Out from his coffin, Drac's voice did
  ring
Seems he was troubled by just one
  thing
He opened the lid and shook his fist
And said, "Whatever happened to my
  Transylvanian twist?"

It's now the mash
It's now the monster mash
The monster mash
And it's a graveyard smash
It's now the mash
It's caught on in a flash
It's now the mash
It's now the monster mash.

Now everything's cool, Drac's a part
  of the band
And my monster mash is the hit of the
  land
For you, the living, this mash was
  meant too
When you get to my door, tell them
  Boris sent you

Then you can mash
Then you can monster mash
The monster mash
And do my graveyard smash
Then you can mash
You'll catch on in a flash
Then you can mash
Then you can monster mash.

I'M HENRY VIII, I AM

Herman's Hermits

#30

━━━━━━━━━ FOR THE RECORD ━━━━━━━━━

Released by MGM Records in 1965.
Playing time: 1:49.
Was #1 on the *Billboard* Hot 100 for one week.
Was a gold single.

━━━━━━━━━ BACKGROUND MUSIC ━━━━━━━━━

"I'm Henry VIII, I Am" was written long before rock and roll. In fact, it was an obscure turn-of-the-century English music hall ditty that Herman's Hermits rediscovered when they were looking through old sheet music.

The group was searching for tunes from way back when because—for reasons which they couldn't fathom—American teens seemed to groove on updated versions of old English music hall songs. At least, fans did with the Herman's Hermits' contemporary but nostalgic-sounding hit "Mrs. Brown You've Got a Lovely Daughter."

Peter Noone, leader of the group, attended Manchester School of Music in England to study drama, music and singing. In 1963, at the age of 16, he teamed up with some friends to form a rock band called the Heartbeats, a name that was soon changed to Herman's Hermits. They performed at youth clubs, teen dance halls, and various social functions.

Although Noone loved rock, he also took a fancy to old English tunes. One day, he heard a song in a British TV play that sounded like a London music hall ditty even though it had been written only a year earlier. After much persuading, he convinced the band to include it in their act. Called "Mrs. Brown You've Got a Lovely Daughter," the song was perfect for weddings and bar mitzvahs, where Noone would change the name to fit the occasion: "Mrs. Smith you've got a lovely daughter."

A year later, the band's two agents sent record producer Mickie Most a plane ticket to Manchester to watch Herman's Hermits perform on stage. The producer thought that Noone looked like a teenage version of President John F. Kennedy and that the singer's "little boy lost" look made him an ideal frontman for the band.

After Most signed up the group in 1964, they debuted with "I'm Into Something Good" which peaked at #19 in England. It did even better in the United States where it climbed to

#13, selling over a million copies.

"The first time I heard my song on the radio, I rolled around on the floor," Noone said in the book *Behind the Hits*. "It wasn't even a clean floor . . . I was in a little club and there was a big bag of onions. I was so excited that I took this bag of onions and I threw one through every window in the warehouse [across a canal from the club] . . . It's funny how happiness made me want to destroy windows. I just went crazy . . . Elvis was on the radio. The Beatles were on the radio. And now *I* was on the radio!"

When they were in the studio recording their first album, "Introducing Herman's Hermits," the group ran out of material but still had room for one more song. "So the twelfth track became 'Mrs. Brown' because it was the easiest and quickest one to record," Noone recalled.

MGM Records chose to release "Silhouettes"—an updating of the Rays' 1958 hit—as the first single from the album. Although stations played it, DJs were even more enthusiastic about "Mrs. Brown" and played that cut off the album. The song received so much airplay that MGM was forced to bring it out as a single. It quickly soared to #1.

"Because of 'Mrs. Brown,' all of a sudden, people in America wanted to hear a different kind of English sound that was not from the Beatles," Noone recalled. "They wanted the sound of the old music hall songs, so we went looking for them. We went to all these old publishers and got all the old songs out and the one that we thought was the best was 'I'm Henery the Eighth, I Am.'" The song, written in 1911, was popularized by music hall comedian Harry Champion.

Although the group had the music, they didn't have the words. "We couldn't remember how it went," Noone said. "We went into the studio and tried it, and that's where that 'Second verse, same as the first' came from . . . There are many verses—but I could only remember one, so I just kept doing it. And it's not even the verse. It's the chorus!"

NOTEWORTHY NOTES

- The Hermits didn't actually play on their studio recordings. The music was left in the hands of session musicians. Among those who backed Peter Noone's vocals on the records were Jimmy Page and John Paul Jones—who, together, later founded Led Zeppelin.

- "I'm Henry VIII, I Am" knocked the Rolling Stones' "(I Can't Get No) Satisfaction" off the top of the chart in the U.S.

- Although it was a #1 hit in the United States, the song was not released in Great Britain because it was considered too ethnic.

- At the time the record came out, Peter Noone was voted one of the ten best-dressed men in the United Kingdom.

Michael Ochs Archives

■ Herman's Hermits could be seen in a cameo appearance in the teen movie *When the Boys Meet the* *Girls*, starring Connie Francis and Harve Presnell. It came out immediately before the song was released.

PLATTER PATTER

Herman's Hermits got their name thanks, in part, to a popular cartoon show on television.

The group started out as the Heartbeats, with Noone singing under the name of Peter Novak. But within a few months, the band changed its name.

It happened after Karl Green, who played bass, noted that Noone closely resembled the character Sherman in the "The Rocky and Bullwinkle Show." (Sherman was the adopted son of Mr. Peabody, a wealthy talking dog with whom he traveled back in time.) The band members started calling Noone "Sherman," which somehow turned into "Herman." They changed the name of the group to Herman and His Hermits, which was then shortened to Herman's Hermits.

FOLLOW UPS AND DOWNS

Herman's Hermits racked up six more Top 10 songs after "I'm Henery the Eighth, I Am." They were: "Just a Little Bit Better," #7 in 1965; "A Must To Avoid," #8, "Listen People," #3, "Leaning on the Lamp Post," #9, "Dandy," #5, all in 1966; and "There's a Kind of Hush," #4 in 1967.

ROCK ON

Peter Noone split from the group in 1972 to write and sing on his own. He opened a clothing shop in New York called the Zoo Boutique and later formed a new group, the Tremblers, which failed to make the charts. In 1983, he received critical acclaim for his acting in the London version of the Broadway hit "The Pirates of Penzance." He later became a veejay on VH1 and host of the network's show "My Generation."

Meanwhile, the Herman-less Hermits have continued to tour regularly.

I'm Henery the Eighth, I Am*

I'm Henery the Eighth I am!
Henery the Eighth I am, I am!
I got married to the widow next door
She's been married seven times before.
Ev'ry one was a Henery, she wouldn't
have a Willy or a Sam.
I'm her eighth old man named Henery,
I'm Henery the Eighth, I am!

* Original lyrics of the old English music hall hit.

KOOKIE, KOOKIE (LEND ME YOUR COMB)

Edd Byrnes and Connie Stevens

#29

───────── FOR THE RECORD ─────────

Released by Warner Brothers Records in 1959.
Playing time: 2:05.
Reached #4 on the *Billboard* Hot 100.
Sold over one million copies.

───────── BACKGROUND MUSIC ─────────

A jive-talking character on one of TV's biggest hits in the late fifties parlayed his habit of constantly combing his hair into a smash novelty tune.

Edd Byrnes portrayed Gerald Lloyd Kookson III—Kookie for short—on "77 Sunset Strip," a glamorous private eye show based in Hollywood. It starred Efrem Zimbalist Jr. as a suave, former intelligence officer and Roger Smith, a former government agent with a law degree.

Next door to their office was Dino's restaurant where Kookie, who longed to be a detective himself and often helped the gumshoes, worked as a parking lot attendant. Kookie provided the show's comic relief with his trademark hip lingo, tossing off such phrases such as: "the ginchiest" (the greatest), "piling up the Z's" (sleeping), "keep the eyeballs rolling" (be on the lookout), "play like a pigeon" (deliver a message), and "a dark seven," (a bad week). But what audiences—especially teenage girls—found most appealing about Kookie was that he constantly combed his thick, dark blond hair. Thanks in no small measure to the way Edd Byrnes played Kookie, the show vaulted into the top ten shortly after it debuted on ABC in 1958—and it spun off a hit record.

Byrnes' rise from obscurity to stardom in TV and music reads like a classic Hollywood rags-to-riches success story. Growing up in a poor New York neighborhood, Byrnes loved reading fan magazine articles about how actors from underprivileged backgrounds had soared to stardom through sheer bravado and determination. He decided he could do that, too.

He quit his part-time jobs as an ambulance driver, roofer, and salesman in a flower shop. Then he badgered a friend into getting him a nonpaying job with an obscure summer stock company in Connecticut in 1956. "Believe it or not, I started getting acting parts in the company," he told *Time* magazine. "Some of them were pretty big. Then I started making the rounds in New York for acting jobs that paid. I went from door to door. I tried Broadway. I tried television. I tried everything. They would tell me I was no good because I had a New York accent, or because I had no experience, or because nobody knew me."

After a year of getting nowhere, Byrnes—with only $110 in his pocket—drove out west in 1956 to conquer Hollywood. He was convinced his self-confidence and cockiness would make up for his lack of experience. He even distributed photos of himself with a fake list of acting credits in hopes of landing an agent. It didn't work.

Down to his last few dollars after pawning everything he had, Byrnes joined a small acting company that paid him $22.50 a week. He boarded with a family for $8 a week and lived mainly on hot dogs and hamburgers.

One day, about six months after he had arrived in Hollywood, he was in his car at a stop light when he recognized an agent in the auto next to him. Byrnes flipped a photo and resume into the agent's open window and sped off. The next day, the agent called, praised him for his nerve, signed him up, and found him work in small bit parts in movies and television.

Byrnes finally got his big break when he auditioned and won the part of Kookie in the pilot for "77 Sunset Strip." Within weeks after the series first aired, Byrnes' character caught the public's fancy. Girls thought he was cute; guys thought he was cool; and mothers thought he was neat and set a good example for youngsters because he always combed his hair.

In one of the first episodes, Kookie helped catch a jewel thief by staging a revue in which he sang a song about combing his hair. Warner Brothers, which produced the TV show, discovered that teens loved the song, so the studio signed Byrnes to a record deal.

The producers teamed him up with Connie Stevens, who had started her singing career with a Los Angeles group called the Three Debs. She also had just been cast to play in another Warner Brothers detective show called "Hawaiian Eye," in which she played Cricket Blake, a somewhat addled photographer who moonlighted as a singer.

On the record, Stevens, in a sweet, marshmallow voice, implores Kookie over and over to "lend me your comb," while he responds to her in the jive lingo of the day. The song became such a smash that Byrnes soon began to overshadow the two stars of "77 Sunset Strip."

In fact, when the TV producers refused to meet his demand to have a bigger role on the show, Byrnes walked out. He was replaced by Troy Donahue, who played a long-haired bookworm. Eventually, Byrnes returned and Kookie was made a full partner in the detective firm for the final three years of the series, which ended in the summer of 1964.

Michael Ochs Archives

NOTEWORTHY NOTES

- As a promotion for the record, Warner Brothers negotiated a deal with a comb manufacturer to turn out hundreds of thousands of "Kookie Kombs."
- Within a month after the song was released, Byrnes had received more than a thousand combs from fans.
- When a Los Angeles DJ casually asked listeners, "Should Kookie cut his hair?", the phone lines lit up. Of the more than 5,000 calls that came in, only 50 suggested that Kookie clip his locks.
- Byrnes was born with the unhip name of Edward Breitenberger. He changed his first name to Edd because, he said, "Edward is too formal and there are lots of Eddies." He chose his new last name be-

cause he wanted something that wasn't "squaresville."

- Feeling somewhat jealous over Byrnes' musical success, costar Roger Smith put out his own album called "Beach Romance." It bombed.

FOLLOW UPS AND DOWNS

Kookie, Kookie (Lend Me Your Comb)" was Edd Byrnes' only big hit. He followed it up that same year with another duet, "Like I Love You," which peaked at #42. He sang the song with Joanie Sommers, who later would have a #7 hit with "Johnny Got Angry" in 1962.

Byrnes also recorded "Hot Rod Rock," "Saturday Night on Sunset Strip," and "The Kookie Cha Cha Cha"—none of which made it onto the charts.

Connie Stevens recorded her biggest hit in 1960 with "16 Reasons," which climbed to #3.

ROCK ON

Byrnes found it almost impossible to shake his Kookie image and wound up playing small roles in B movies like *The Secret Invasion* in 1964 and *Beach Ball* in 1965. He then moved to Europe where he acted in spaghetti westerns before returning to Hollywood. Over the years, Byrnes has guested on TV shows and had bit parts in other films, including *Grease* in 1978. He hasn't cut a record since the early 1960s.

Meanwhile, Stevens went on to a successful career as a character actress in movies and television and as a nightclub entertainer. She's made millions of dollars with her line of skin care products—Forever Spring for women and Kiyak for men—which she pitches on the Home Shopping Network.

Kookie, Kookie (Lend Me Your Comb)

Connie: Kookie, Kookie, lend me your comb.
Kookie, Kookie.
Kookie: Well now, let's take it from the top and grab some wheels.
We'll wail along and talk about some coo coo deals.
Connie: But Kookie, Kookie, lend me your comb.
Kookie, Kookie.
Kookie: Now you're on my wave length and I'm readin' you just fine.
Don't cut out of here till we get on cloud nine.
Connie: But Kookie, Kookie.
Kookie: I've got smog in my noggin ever since you made the scene.
Connie: You're the utmost.
Kookie: If you ever tune me out, Dad, I'm the saddest. Like I'm green.
Connie: The very utmost. Kookie, Kookie, lend me your comb.
Kookie, Kookie.
Kookie: Man, I've got my burners lighted and my flaps are gonna bend.
You're gonna send me to that planet

called, you know it, baby, The End.
Connie: But Kookie, Kookie, lend me your comb.
Kookie, Kookie.
Kookie: If you ever cut out, then I'd be a stray cat
'Cause when I'm flying solo, nowhere's where I'm at.
Connie: But Kookie, Kookie, lend me your comb.
Kookie, Kookie.
Kookie: What's with this comb caper, baby?
Why do you wanna latch on to my comb?
Connie: I just want you to stop combing your hair and kiss me.
You're the maximum utmost.
Kookie: Well, I'm beamed in on Dreamsville and I'm moving right now,
'Cause that's the kind of scene that I dig.
Baby, you're the ginchiest!

YAKETY YAK
The Coasters

#28

━━━━━━━ FOR THE RECORD ━━━━━━━

Released by Atco Records in 1958.
Playing time: 1:50.
Soared to #1 on the *Billboard* Hot 100.

━━━━━━━ BACKGROUND MUSIC ━━━━━━━

"**Y**akety Yak"—a tune poking fun at parents' insistence that kids do their chores—was a spur-of-the-moment song that took all of ten minutes to write.

It came from the creative minds of the songwriting team of Jerry Leiber and Mike Stoller.

The two first met in school in Los Angeles in 1950 when they were 17. The youngsters had much in common: they were Jewish, they dated black girls, and they loved blues.

Together, they began writing and selling songs. "We used to go to Mike's house where the upright piano was," said Leiber. "We went there every day and wrote. We worked 12 hours a day."

Added Stoller, "We'd write five songs at a session. Then Jerry would go home, and we'd call each other up. 'I've written six more songs!' 'I've written four more!'"

By the time they turned 20, Leiber and Stoller headed their own record label, Spark Records, and wrote for black singers and groups. "I felt

black," Leiber once told *Rolling Stone*. "I *was* black as far as I was concerned. And I wanted to be black for lots of reasons. They were better musicians, they were better athletes, they were not uptight about sex, and they knew how to enjoy life better than most people. Mike and I lived a black lifestyle as young guys. We had black girlfriends for years."

Among the first groups they wrote and produced for were the Robins, who scored two local hits including "Riot in Cell Block #9" and "Smokey Joe's Cafe." Then Leiber and Stoller cut a deal with Atlantic Records to issue their songs. When some of the Robins flew the coop for another label, Carl Gardner, Billy Guy, Leon Hughes, and Bobby Nunn became the Coasters.

After their first chart song, "One Kiss Led To Another," stalled at #73 in 1956, the Coasters found success in 1957 with "Searchin'" (#3) and "Young Blood" (#8)—all written by Leiber (the lyrics) and Stoller (the music).

"When we started to write, we

were writing to amuse ourselves," Stoller said. "And we got very lucky in the sense that at some point what we wrote also amused a lot of other people."

The writing duo created the Coasters' style of telling an urban story with an appealing blend of R&B and comedy.

Or, as Leiber once called it, "a white kid's view of a black person's conception of white society." The song that epitomized this style was the light-hearted "Yakety Yak."

"It was written very quickly," said Leiber. "I had this beautiful little duplex on Washington Square in the Village right off the park. Mike came over one afternoon to work and he sat down at the piano."

Added Stoller, "Jerry was boiling some water to make tea, and I was playing a rhythm that struck me as being funny—kind of in the mood of the Coasters. Jerry started yelling, 'Take out the papers and the trash!' And then I yelled out, 'Or you don't get no spendin' cash!' And that was it. We knew we had something."

Leiber said it was like automatic writing. "The song just wrote itself. It was over in ten minutes. There's nothing more perfect than those that come out that way."

Although the song sounded lively and spontaneous, everything on the record was plotted to the millisecond.

As they did for all their songs, Leiber and Stoller performed the song for the artists first and then had the group rehearse relentlessly every day. "We would tailor the material to the individual singers," said Stoller. "It was like a radio play, and we had written a scored script—how and when they came in, if there was a pause, whether it was a second or a half second. Everything was rehearsed."

Leiber said they wrote "Yakety Yak" specifically for the Coasters because of the singers' personalities. "The bass singers were always rather laid back, but their voices always carried some kind of authority—a dark, semi-sinister, semi-comic authority," Leiber said. "They were the heavies in our comic melodramas. Carl Gardner had such an absurdly pompous way of expressing himself. Billy Guy was the sort of mischievous rube. They were almost like characters out of a comic strip, and they always played the same role."

With Guy and Gardner singing lead vocals, Stoller playing the piano, King Curtis providing the famous saxophone work, and five other musicians backing them, "Yakety Yak" became The Coasters' first and only #1 hit.

NOTEWORTHY NOTES

- Mike Stoller and his wife, Meryl, were passengers on the Italian ocean liner *Andrea Doria* when it collided with the Swedish liner *Stockholm* off the coast of Nantucket in 1956. The couple managed to make it to the safety of a lifeboat before their ship sank. The disaster claimed the lives of 51 fellow passengers.

- Jerry Leiber's son Oliver followed in his footsteps by becoming a songwriter and producer. Oliver wrote and produced the Paula Abdul #1 hits "Forever Your Girl" and "Opposites Attract."

FOLLOW UPS AND DOWNS

"Yakety Yak" was followed up in 1959 with three rhythm and blues playlets that all became Top Ten hits: "Charlie Brown," #2; "Along Came Jones," #9; and "Poison Ivy," #7.

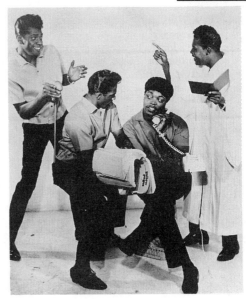

Showtime Archives

ROCK ON

After writing hits in the fifties and early sixties for the Coasters and such stars as Elvis Presley, the Drifters, and Ben E. King, Jerry Leiber and Mike Stoller oversaw the rise of top girl groups like the Dixie Cups and the Shangri-Las, produced records for Procol Harum, and scored a number of movies.

As for the Coasters, tragedy struck several former and newer members. In 1961, saxophonist King Curtis was stabbed to death outside his apartment. In 1980, bass singer Nathaniel "Buster" Wilson was shot and killed, his body dismembered and dumped near Hoover Dam. Six years later, Bobby Nunn died of a heart attack. In 1990, tenor Cornelius Gunter was gunned down in his car.

In 1987, Leiber and Stoller and the Coasters were inducted into the Rock and Roll Hall of Fame.

Yakety Yak

Take out the papers and the trash
Or you don't get no spendin' cash
If you don't scub that kitchen floor
You ain't gonna rock 'n' roll no more

Yakety yak
Don't talk back

Just finish cleanin' up your room
Let's see that dust fly with that broom
Get all that garbage out of sight
Or you don't go out Friday night

Yakety yak
Don't talk back

You just put on your coat and hat
And walk yourself to the laundromat
And when you finish doing that
Bring in the dog and put out the cat

Yakety yak
Don't talk back

Don't you give me no dirty looks
Your father's hip, he knows what cooks
Just tell your hoodlum friends outside
You ain't got time to take a ride.

Yakety yak
Don't talk back

CHUG-A-LUG
Roger Miller

#27

FOR THE RECORD

Released by Smash Records in 1964.
Playing time: 2:00
Peaked at #9 on the Billboard Hot 100.

BACKGROUND MUSIC

Roger Miller's zany tune about the fun—and consequences—of a youngster's first taste of booze was taken from his own childhood experience.

"There's something about that first sip of grape wine, moonshine, and bottled liquor that you never forget," the country star once said. "It stays with you a lot longer than the buzz you get from that stuff."

Almost all of Miller's hits had an autobiographical tinge to them. He was only an infant when his father died and his poverty-stricken mother found herself unable to support Roger and his two brothers. So she sent each of her sons to a different relative to raise. Roger ended up with an aunt and uncle on a farm with no electricity near Erick, Oklahoma. There, he milked cows in the morning, walked three miles to a one-room schoolhouse, and worked the cotton fields when he got home.

When he was 12 years old, Miller took the $8 he earned from picking 400 pounds of cotton and bought a used guitar. He taught himself how to play the instrument—as well as the fiddle, banjo, piano, and drums—because he was convinced that music could lead him out of his dreary life. "I used to say, 'Lord, give me a guitar and let me get out of here and make something of the world,'" he once told *Newsday*. "I just wanted to get away from the manure."

Miller quit school at the age of 14 and bummed around Texas and Oklahoma, working odd jobs that included cattle herding, tractor driving, and bronco riding in rodeos. He also played his guitar in local clubs before signing up for a three-year stint in the Army in Korea where he drove a jeep and performed in a Special Services country band.

One of Miller's sergeants was the brother of Jethro, of the famed country duo Homer and Jethro, who suggested that Roger try his luck in Nashville after his discharge. At his first audition with RCA Records, Miller was so nervous that he sang in one key and played in another. He was a bust, and went back to doing odd jobs, including working as a bellhop at a swank Nashville hotel.

But he never gave up his dream of making a name for himself in the music world. During the late 1950s, Miller worked as a drummer for Faron Young, fiddled for Minnie Pearl, and played guitar for George Jones. He also wrote songs and spent a lot of time "walking the streets of Nashville, trying to get anybody to record my songs."

He wrote his first hit in 1958 when Ray Price recorded Miller's "Invitation to the Blues," which made it to #25. After writing more than 150 country tunes—many of which were recorded—Miller was still looking for the big hit that would put him on the map. In 1964, he recorded "Dang Me," which became a million-seller, rising as high as at #7.

Then came "Chug-A-Lug." Miller, who was no stranger to booze, recalled the days as a youngster when he used to find a stash of home-made wine in a Mason jar and drink it with a buddy. Occasionally, he and his pals would uncover bottles of high-octane moonshine by a hidden still. He also remembered the terrible hangovers he felt the next day after guzzling the hooch. So he decided to compose "Chug-A-Lug"—and, like "Dang Me," it became another huge hit.

The song vaulted beyond the boundaries of country music and into mainstream pop, making Miller a full-fledged star.

At the height of his fame, the singer explained to the press why he didn't want to be labeled strictly a country and western star: "I prefer to go in my own direction and let someone follow me."

NOTEWORTHY NOTES

- One of Miller's earliest musical influences was his cousin by marriage, Sheb Wooley, who composed and sang the novelty tune "The Purple People Eater."

- After recording "Dang Me" and "Chug-A-Lug," Miller won a Grammy for Best New Country and Western Artist.

- Miller seldom wrote down the songs he sang. He would keep the song in his head and when he was ready to record it, he would sing the tune to the session musicians over and over until they learned it.

- He starred in his own musical variety network TV show in 1966. Unfortunately, "The Roger Miller Show" lasted only four months. He blamed its failure on the producers who "were trying to make a country Andy Williams out of me."

FOLLOW UPS AND DOWNS

Miller followed up his back-to-back hits with "Do-Wacka-Do," #31, and "Engine, Engine Number Nine," #7, both in 1965. That same year, he recorded his biggest smash, "King of the Road," which reached #4 and sold over 2.5 million records. "King of the Road" has been re-corded by more than 300 artists in 30 different languages.

Among other irreverent, fun songs he wrote and recorded were "You Can't Roller Skate in a Buffalo Herd," "My Uncle Used To Love Me But She Died," and "(The Day I Jumped) From Uncle Harvey's Plane."

ROCK ON

At the peak of his popularity, Miller plunged into the pits of despair as the result of a substance abuse problem, which halted his career and ruined his first two marriages. Eventually, he beat his addiction to alcohol and amphetamines.

In the early 1980s, Miller, with a fresh start and a new wife, started touring and recording again and discovered a whole new generation of fans who loved his wacky tunes.

He received critical acclaim after writing the music for the 1985 Broadway hit *Big River*. (During part of its 2-year run, he made his stage acting debut by playing the drunken father of Huckleberry Finn.)

He continued to write songs until 1990 when doctors discovered he was suffering from throat cancer. Despite aggressive treatment, the cancer spread and Miller died in 1992.

PHOTO COURTESY: Michael Ochs Archives

Chug-A-Lug

Chug-a-lug, chug-a-lug
Makes ya wanta holler hi-de-ho.
Burns your tummy, don't you know.
Chug-a-lug, chug-a-lug.

Grape wine in a mason jar,
Homemade and brought to school
By a friend of mine. After class
Me and him and this other fool
Decide that we'll drink up what's left.
Chug-a-lug, so we helped ourselves.
First time for everything.
Ummm, my ears still ring.

Chug-a-lug, chug-a-lug
Makes ya wanta holler hi-de-ho.
Burns your tummy, don't you know.
Chug-a-lug, chug-a-lug.

4-H and F.F.A.
On a field trip to the farm.
Me and a friend sneak off behind
This big old barn
Where we uncovered a covered-up
*   moonshine still*
And we thought we'd drink our fill
And swallered it with a smile.
I ran ten miles.

Chug-a-lug, chug-a-lug
Makes ya wanta holler hi-de-ho.
Burns your tummy, don't you know.
Chug-a-lug, chug-a-lug.

Jukebox and a sawdust floor
Somethin' like I never seen.
Heck, I'm just goin' on fifteen.
But with the help of
My finaglin' uncle I got snuck in
For my first real taste of sin.
I said, "Let me have a big ole sip!"
I done a double back flip.

Chug-a-lug, chug-a-lug
Makes ya wanta holler hi-de-ho.
Burns your tummy, don't you know.
Chug-a-lug, chug-a-lug.

EAT IT
"Weird Al" Yankovic

#26

━━━━━━━━ FOR THE RECORD ━━━━━━━━

Released by Rock 'n' Roll Records in 1984.
Playing time: 3:19.
Climbed as high as #12 on the *Billboard* Hot 100.
Went to #1 in Australia.
Earned a Grammy for Best Comedy Recording.

━━━━━━━━ BACKGROUND MUSIC ━━━━━━━━

Always willing to take a poke (or a polka) at the rock establishment, accordion-playing funnyman "Weird Al" Yankovic spoofed one of the music world's biggest stars, Michael Jackson—but only after the King of Pop gave his blessing. As a result, the Clown Prince of Parody scored his biggest hit ever with "Eat It."

"Weird Al" said he always wanted to play in a rock and roll band, "but when my parents were making life-altering decisions for me, they handed me an accordion. With an accordion, well, polka tends to follow right along. Because they don't teach 'In-a-Gadda-da-Vida' when you're taking accordion lessons, I grew up learning 'The Beer Barrel Polka' and other things like that."

At the age of 15, "Weird Al," who often played at weddings and bar mitzvahs, began writing parodies, recording them on a cheap cassette player and sending them to "The Dr. Demento Show," the popular syndicated radio program featuring music's most bizarre recordings. To Yankovic's surprise, Dr. Demento played his songs on the show, including takeoffs of Queen's "Another One Bites the Dust" (called "Another One Rides the Bus") and Barbra Streisand and Neil Diamond's "You Don't Bring Me Flowers" (called "You Don't Take Showers").

Later, while studying architecture at Cal Poly San Luis Obispo, "Weird Al" took a shot at the Knack's hit "My Sharona." The result: "My Bologna," a song he recorded in the bathroom across the hall from the campus radio station. Shortly after Dr. Demento began airing it, the Knack came to the school for a concert. "Weird Al" met them backstage and played the band his spoof. They liked it so much that they introduced him to an executive from their record company. "Capitol Records decided right there to put out the single," Yankovic recalled. "But they didn't promote it or even re-record it. They put out the original bathroom recording. I think they just didn't want to incur any recording debts on it. It was a one-shot thing."

While working in the mail room of a radio syndication company following graduation, "Weird Al" continued to write shrewd parodies that Dr. Demento played on his show. The songs eventually led to a recording contract for his first album, "'Weird Al' Yankovic."

While on tour, he and his band sang what he called his Fabulous Food Medley, including "My Bologna," "Spameater" (a parody of "Maneater"), "Avocado" (a takeoff of "Desperado"), and "A Whole Lotta Lunch" (a send-up of "Whole Lotta Love"). Also included was a wacky chorus of "Eat It" from Michael Jackson's monster 1983 hit "Beat It."

"We got such a great reaction from the audience that I thought we should fill it out to an entire song," Yankovic recalled. "So we approached Michael Jackson and gave him the first chorus that we'd written and asked what he'd think of us doing this song. He was very open to it, so I wrote out the entire song and sent it to him and he gave us his final approval. I guess we got him at the right time. He was very receptive and very nice about it and he had a great sense of humor. He's not only a good target for parody, but also a very good sport."

NOTEWORTHY NOTES

- Michael Jackson is listed as the co-writer on "Eat It." Said Yankovic, "It's crazy—he's making money off of me! Good bucks, in fact."

- "Weird Al" lampooned Michael Jackson's video of "Beat It" with his own letter-perfect send-up, in which he boldly intervenes in a gang war fought over a rubber chicken. Yankovic won an American Video Award as Best Male Performer, beating out Bruce Springsteen and George Michael.

PLATTER PATTER

"Weird Al" once tried out for "The Gong Show," but he flunked his audition. "I played the accordion and sang a song called 'Mr. Frump in the Iron Lung,'" he recalled. "I don't know, I guess they thought it was in poor taste."

He portrayed an alien in a 1985 episode of Steven Spielberg's TV series "Amazing Stories." Yankovic was a cabbage man from outer space. "I had a leafy green moustache and strange-looking glasses," he said. "It took three hours every morning to get into makeup."

FOLLOW UPS AND DOWNS

"Weird Al" followed up his success of "Eat It" with a new album in 1985, "Dare To Be Stupid," in which he parodied more popular songs of the day: "Like a Virgin" by Madonna ("Like a Surgeon"), "I Want a New Drug" by Huey Lewis ("I Want a New Duck"), and "Lola" by the Kinks ("Yoda"). The next year brought Yankovic's "Polka Party!" which included the James Brown parody "Living with a Hernia," the Robert Palmer send-up "Addicted to Spuds," and the cheery yuletide anthem "Christmas at Ground Zero." Then, in 1988, his album "Even Worse" did takeoffs of songs by Michael Jackson ("Fat"), George Harrison ("This Song's Just Six Words Long"), Los Lobos ("Lasa-

PHOTO COURTESY: Scotti Brothers

gna") and Billy Idol ("Alimony"). His latest album, "Off the Deep End," lampoons songs by Nirvana, Hammer, New Kids on the Block, and Milli Vanilli.

ROCK ON

The Weird One continues to write parodies, record albums, and tour. "My concerts are like a Prince concert—only intentionally funny," he said.

His latest tour featured a high-energy mix of hilarious videos, costume changes and, of course, a medley of rock songs done polka style. "I play the accordion and do songs in the style

in which I think they were originally intended to be heard," he said.

"I still think that polka is the new wave of the future, and people like Madonna and Prince are going to fall by the wayside. The new heroes of pop culture are going to be people like Frank Yankovic, Little Wally, Eddie Lazanchak, and the Versatones, people like that."

Eat It

*How come you're always such a fussy
    young man
Don't want no Captain Crunch
Don't want no Raisin Bran
Well don't you know that other kids
Are starving in Japan
So eat it
Just eat it*

*Don't want to argue, I don't want to
    debate
Don't want to hear about
What kind of food you hate
You won't get no dessert
Till you clean off your plate
So eat it
Don't tell me you're full*

*Just eat it, eat it
Get yourself an egg and beat it
Have some more chicken
Have some more pie
It doesn't matter
If it's boiled or fried
Just eat it, just eat it
Just eat it, just eat it.*

*Your table manners are a crying shame
You're playing with your food
This ain't some kind of game
Now if you starve to death
You'll just have yourself to blame
So eat it
Just eat it*

*You better listen, better do what
    you're told
You haven't even touched
Your tuna casserole*

*You better chow down
Or it's gonna get cold
So eat it
I don't care if you're full*

*Just eat it, eat it
Open up your mouth and feed it
Have some more yogurt
Have some more Spam
It doesn't matter
If it's fresh or canned*

*Just eat it, eat it
Don't you make me repeat it
Have a banana
Have a whole bunch
It doesn't matter
What you had for lunch
Just eat it, eat it
Eat it, eat it
Eat it, eat it
Eat it, eat it*

*Eat it, eat it
If it's getting cold, reheat it
Have a big dinner
Have a light snack
If you don't like it
You can send it back*

*Just eat it, eat it
Get yourself an egg and beat it
Have some more chicken
Have some more pie
It doesn't matter
If it's boiled or fried
Just eat it
Eat it*

Y.M.C.A.
Village People

FOR THE RECORD

Released by Casablanca Records in 1978.
Playing time: 3:30.
Made it to #2 on the *Billboard* Hot 100 in 1979 and remained there for three weeks.
Was a platinum single, selling 2 million copies in the U.S. and 12 million worldwide.

BACKGROUND MUSIC

This campy, tongue-in-cheek ode to the Y.M.C.A. was an afterthought, written at the last minute because the Village People were short one song on the album they were making. It turned out to be the biggest hit ever for the group that made a living parodying male stereotypes.

In 1977, French composer-producer Jacques Morali moved to New York, where he became fascinated with the gay disco scene. He told *Rolling Stone* in a 1979 interview that he was intrigued with the way men dressed up in macho costumes and danced together in Greenwich Village discos. "After that I said to myself, 'You know, this is fantastic—to see the cowboy, the Indian, the construction worker with other men around.'" So he decided to create an imaginary disco group called the Village People.

Morali wrote songs aimed at the gay market, produced an album with session musicians, and designed a cover featuring beefcake models

dressed in macho costumes. The LP, "Village People," created excitement in the gay discos—and then crossed over into pop radio. That was the good news. The bad news was that Morali had no group to hit the road and do personal appearances to promote the record.

Eventually, Morali hired Victor Willis, who had sung in two Broadway shows (the cop); Felipe Rose, a professional dancer (the Indian); singer Alex Briley (the GI); TV actor Randy Jones (the cowboy); Glenn Hughes, a former Brooklyn toll collector (the leather-clad biker); and David Hodo, who roller skated while eating fire on TV's "What's My Line?" (the construction worker).

After overcoming scathing reviews (one critic called them a "faggot high school band"), the Village People watched their popularity soar among gays *and* straights—especially after "Macho Man" came out in 1978. Morali said he wrote the song "believing that the gay audiences were going to like it very much. But the straight audiences liked the song much more, because straight guys in America want to get the macho look." The song peaked at #25.

Then came the People's big hit, "Y.M.C.A."

"The song was an afterthought," recalled Glenn Hughes. "We were working on our album, 'Cruisin',' and the whole push for that album was going to be the single 'The Women.' We spent a lot of time on that song because the producers thought it would be a good follow-up to 'Macho Man.'

"At some point, they realized we were one song short for the album. So one day Jacques was walking down the street in New York and saw a sign that said 'Y.M.C.A.' and he asked a friend, 'What's that?' And his friend said, 'That's the Young Men's Christian Association.' Jacques went, 'Hmmm, young men, huh?' He went home and 20 minutes later he had finished writing the song.

"When he brought it to the studio, we thought it was hysterical. To us, it was just a throwaway. But then after the album was produced, the record company released 'Y.M.C.A.' as the single."

The Y.M.C.A. didn't know how to take the song at first.

The lyrics seemed innocent enough. Yet a few Y officials were convinced that between the lines lurked homosexual overtones. Some enlightened Y's, recognizing the publicity bonanza, invited the Village People to do shows. But the top brass of the Y.M.C.A. squashed the idea.

What ticked off the Y.M.C.A. the most was that the Village People, their producers, and Casablanca Records never bothered to ask the organization if it was okay to use the Y.M.C.A. trademark and name. Eventually, the matter of trademark infringement was settled and the Y.M.C.A. realized that the song was basically a free commercial.

As David Hodo told reporters back then, "We put Y.M.C.A. on everybody's tongue after 75 years of cobwebs." Then, with a grin, he added, "We're sticking our tongue in society's cheek."

NOTEWORTHY NOTES

- Glenn Hughes, the leather-clad biker, said he auditioned for the group on a dare. "I went as a joke, and even though I hadn't sung professionally, I got the job."

- On tour, lead singer Victor Willis used a live mike while the other People lip-synched over taped music.

- In 1980, the group starred in the feature film *Can't Stop the Music*—which showcased "Y.M.C.A." The movie bombed big time.

—— PLATTER ——
PATTER

The custom of the audience spelling out the letters Y-M-C-A with their hands and arms while the the Village People performed the song was dreamed up by Dick Clark.

In September, 1978, America's most famous rock and roll host invited the group to sing "Y.M.C.A." on "American Bandstand" for the first time on television. "Before we played the song, Dick Clark told us, 'The audience has something they want to do for you,'" Glenn Hughes recalled. "So as the song was being played, the audience started dancing and then when we started to

Michael Ochs Archives

sing the chorus 'Y-M-C-A', the audience began doing the hand movements.

"We liked it, so we incorporated it into our act. But we did it only at the end of the song."

———— FOLLOW UPS AND DOWNS ————

The Village People followed up their hit by trying to do for the Navy what they had done for the Y with "In the Navy." The song peaked at #3 in 1979. Then came "Go West" (#45).

Their last charted song, "Ready for the '80s," really wasn't, stalling at #52 and falling off the charts in January, 1980.

———————— ROCK ON ————————

The Village People—minus cop Victor Willis and cowboy Randy Jones, who've been replaced—still perform their high-energy act, mostly on college campuses.

Producer Jacques Morali returned to France in 1984. Seven years later, he died at the age of 44 in Paris from complications brought on by AIDS.

Y.M.C.A.

Young man, there's no need to feel down
I said young man, pick yourself off the
  ground
I said young man, 'cause you're in a
  new town
There's no need to be unhappy.

Young man, there's a place you can go
I said young man, when you're short
  on your dough
You can stay there and I'm sure you
  will find
Many ways to have a good time.

It's fun to stay at the Y.M.C.A.
It's fun to stay at the Y.M.C.A.
They have everything for young men
  to enjoy
You can hang out with all the boys.

It's fun to stay at the Y.M.C.A.
It's fun to stay at the Y.M.C.A.
You can get yourself clean
You can have a good meal
You can do whatever you feel.

Young man, are you listening to me?
I said young man, what do you want
  to be?
I said young man, you can make real
  your dreams
But you've got to know this one thing.

No man does it all by himself
I said young man, put your pride on
  the shelf
And just go there to the Y.M.C.A.
I'm sure they can help you today.

It's fun to stay at the Y.M.C.A.
It's fun to stay at the Y.M.C.A.
They have everything for young men
  to enjoy
You can hang out with all the boys.

It's fun to stay at the Y.M.C.A.
It's fun to stay at the Y.M.C.A.
You can get yourself clean
You can have a good meal
You can do whatever you feel.

Young man, I was once in your shoes
I said, I was down and out and with
  the blues
I felt no man cared if I were alive
I felt the whole world was so jive.

That's when someone came up to me
And said, "Young man, take a walk up
  the street
It's a place there called the Y.M.C.A.
They can start you back on your way."

It's fun to stay at the Y.M.C.A.
It's fun to stay at the Y.M.C.A.
They have everything for young men
  to enjoy
You can hang out with all the boys.

It's fun to stay at the Y.M.C.A.
Young man, young man, there's no
  need to feel down
Young man, young man, pick yourself
  off the ground.

It's fun to stay at the Y.M.C.A.
Young man, young man, I was once in
  your shoes
Young man, young man, I was down
  with the blues.

SUGAR, SUGAR

The Archies

#24

FOR THE RECORD

Released by Calendar Records in 1969.
Playing time: 2:48.
Soared to #1 on the *Billboard* Hot 100 and stayed there for four weeks.
Became a gold single and the top-selling record of the year.

BACKGROUND MUSIC

Milli Vanilli fans, take note: Although the label credits the Archies with singing this classic bubblegum tune, the group never recorded it. That's because they never existed!

Technically, of course, the mischievous, music-loving teens from Riverdale High on the Saturday morning animated TV hit, "The Archie Show," did chart 1969's biggest record. The series was based on the popular "Archie" comic books, featuring Archie, Veronica, Jughead, Betty, and Moose. On each show, the cartoon characters sang new rock songs as a group called the Archies. Several of the tunes were turned into hit records, including the show's biggest smash, "Sugar, Sugar." The truth is, though, most of those songs were sung by one man—Ron Dante.

"I tried to become a solo artist, but my career was going nowhere," Dante said. "So I agreed to become a recording studio ghost and sing anonymously on the Archies' sessions for scale."

Dante started his music career in a painful way—after he broke his arm falling out of a tree. "I had to exercise my wrist, so my dad bought me a guitar," Dante recalled. "I learned how to play it and a year later I formed my first rock group, the Persuaders. I made $50 a night at a time when my dad was making $50 a week. I knew then music would be my life."

By the tender age of 16, Dante was cutting demos for Burt Bacharach, Carole King, and Neil Sedaka and working as a backup musician. In 1964, he was a member of the studio group the Detergents, who sang "Leader of the Laundromat," a spoof of the Shangri-Las' "Leader of the Pack." The novelty tune broke into the Top 20.

Four years later, Dante began fronting for the Archies. Don Kirshner, who helped launch the Monkees, had been hired to supervise the music for the cartoon show. "He was casting for a lead singer and since a friend of mine was playing in the session, I went in and got an audition," Dante recalled.

"I sang for about a half hour and the next day they told me I got the job. We must have done a hundred tunes that first season."

Dante recorded "Bang-Shang-a-Lang" for the show's premiere; when it came out as a single, it climbed up to #22 on the charts. But the next Archies single, "Feelin' So Good (Skooby-Doo)" only made it to #53.

The following year, Dante sang "Sugar, Sugar," which was written by producer Jeff Barry and pop singer Andy Kim. Although the record sounds like Archie and the gang are all singing, the male voices are all Dante's, each one recorded on a separate track. "I sang at least eight or ten parts on 'Sugar, Sugar,'" said Dante. "Toni Wine sang the female parts and Ray Stevens—yes, *the* Ray Stevens—was one of the hand-clappers.

"Most of my friends hated that record and warned me that it could ruin my career because it was so awful. But I liked it. I thought it was cute."

Eight weeks after its release, "Sugar, Sugar" was on the top of the charts.

NOTEWORTHY NOTES

- The Monkees had a chance to record "Sugar, Sugar" two years earlier, but they turned it down.

- Less than a year after the song reached #1, Wilson Pickett recorded a soul version that made it to the Top 25.

PLATTER PATTER

Immediately after recording "Sugar, Sugar," Ron Dante fronted for another fake group called the Cuff Links. He sang all the vocal parts on "their" only hit—"Tracy." Amazingly, the song was in the Top 10 at the same time as "Sugar, Sugar," yet Dante, the artist behind both hits, never received any of the accolades that normally would accompany such a feat.

"It was a funny thing," said Dante. "No one caught on that they were both from the same person."

FOLLOW UPS AND DOWNS

The Archies, or rather Dante, followed up "Sugar, Sugar" with "Jingle Jangle," which reached #10 in 1970.

Then came "Who's Your Baby" (#40) and "Sunshine" (#57) the same year.

Michael Ochs Archives

ROCK ON

Although he thought "Sugar, Sugar" and other Archies tunes were fun music, Dante refused to go out on tour.

"Kids liked the sound, but the Archies weren't a group that went out and performed and won fans," he said. "I was offered big bucks at the time to go out on the road and sing live with the Archies, but I turned it down. I didn't want to be a star under the auspices of a cartoon group."

So Dante continued to carve his niche as an anonymous singer, recording more than 50 commercials—including one that introduced him to a man who would change his life. "In 1972, I recorded a jingle for a new soft drink that tasted like rust and never did make it on the market," he recalled.

"At this session were me and three other unknowns at the time—Barry Manilow, Melissa Manchester, and Valerie Simpson of Ashford and Simpson.

"We all went to lunch and Barry and I hit it off. He played me some songs he had written and I thought they were great. I told him, 'I've never produced anybody, but let's go in on it, pool our resources, and make some records.' Barry wasn't sure if his voice should be on the records because he thought I had a better voice."

Instead, Dante wound up co-producing eight of Manilow's albums before moving on to other projects. Dante has since become a Broadway producer. He continues to produce records and work in music publishing.

Sugar, Sugar

Sugar, ah, honey, honey
You are my candy girl
And you've got me wanting you

Honey, ah, sugar, sugar
You are my candy girl
And you've got me wanting you

I just can't believe
The loveliness of loving you
(I just can't believe it's true)
I just can't believe
The one to love this feeling to
(I just can't believe it's true)

Ah, sugar, ah, honey, honey
You are my candy girl
And you've got me wanting you

Ah, sugar, ah, honey, honey
You are my candy girl
And you've got me wanting you

When I kissed you girl
I knew how sweet a kiss could be
(I know how sweet a kiss can be)
Like the summer sunshine
Pour your sweetness over me
(Pour your sweetness over me)

Oh, sugar
Pour a little sugar on it, honey
Pour a little sugar on it, baby
I'm gonna make your life so sweet
Yeah, yeah, yeah
Pour a little sugar on it, oh yeah

Oh, sugar
Pour a little sugar on it, honey
Pour a little sugar on it, baby
I'm gonna make your life so sweet
Yeah, yeah, yeah
Pour a little sugar on it, honey

Ah, sugar, ah, honey, honey
You are my candy girl
And you got me wanting you

Oh, honey, ah sugar, sugar
You are my candy girl

PLAYGROUND IN MY MIND

Clint Holmes

#23

━━━━━━━━━━ FOR THE RECORD ━━━━━━━━━━

Released by Epic Records in 1972.
Playing time: 2:55.
Reached #2 on the *Billboard* Hot 100 in 1973 and remained there for two weeks.
Was a gold single.

━━━━━━━━━━ BACKGROUND MUSIC ━━━━━━━━━━

This sappy hit about childhood remembrances is also a testament to persistence. The music was the same as that sung by other artists in several songs with different lyrics—songs that all flopped. And when "Playground in My Mind" was released, it, too, bombed—at first.

It was created by prolific writer-producer Paul Vance, who fell in love with the music and was determined to turn it into a hit one way or another.

"We did several different records using the same music," he recalled. "The original title was called 'Mama, Je T' Aime,' which is French for 'Mama, I Love You.' We thought it would be a cute idea to do the background in French. Atlantic Records released it and it died. We came up with other artists and lyrics to go with the music, but it didn't work."

Then Vance thought of making the song about a stressed-out man recalling the carefree days of his childhood, with a little boy singing in the background. To make the record work, Vance needed to find the right male adult voice.

He took a vacation to Paradise Island, Nassau, the Bahamas, where singer Clint Holmes was performing onstage at a casino. Holmes, whose mother was a British opera singer, had become a professional nightclub singer after serving in the U.S. Army chorus in the mid-sixties.

Recalled Vance, "I was gambling in the casino when a friend came over and said, 'Paul, there's a singer named Clint Holmes on stage who's knocking people out.' I said, 'I'm gambling, I'm losing, and I'm not going to look at another artist.' But other people kept telling me how great this guy was, so I said, 'All right, I'll check him out.' I caught his last show and he knocked me down.

"After the show, I went over and introduced myself and said, 'I'd like you to fly to New York when you get a chance and I'll record you.' And he said, 'You know what I am? I'm a cross between Tom Jones and Engelbert Humperdinck.' I told him, 'I don't want to record you like that. I'd like to try a novelty song with you.'

"After I explained 'Playground in My Mind,' he said, 'Oh, no, I couldn't do that . . . unless . . . Would you cut me on other kinds of tunes?' And I replied, 'Yeah, sure, but I think this is going to be a hit.'"

A few weeks later, Holmes went to New York and met with Vance, who played him "Mama, Je T' Aime," which the producer finally conceded was not very good. "Then Clint started singing and I said, 'You're perfect for this!'"

"Clint thought 'Playground' was too bubblegum for him. But because he had such a kind nature about him, he said, 'If you believe in it that much, I'll try it.' So we went into the studio, but it wasn't working out at all."

It just so happened that some of Vance's children and their friends were at the recording session that day. That's when his nine-year-old son Phillip got into the act, recalled Vance. "He asked me, 'Can I sing like I'm the young boy on the record?' I knew the kid couldn't sing and had an attention span of about two minutes, but I said, 'Go ahead.' It was like a joke.

"So he goes in there with Clint and . . . wow! . . . the magic hits and we all knew it the minute the kid opened his mouth. I'm not saying this because he's my son, but without the young kid's voice on there, that record would have gone nowhere. Then I told my daughter and her friends who were at the session, 'Come on. I'll let you

all sing in the background.' They're the ones who sing, 'Ba ba ba ba ba.' They were so real. I mean, there were no professionals in there except Clint. And it was magic because even though those young kids in the background really couldn't sing, they were doing it from their hearts.

"We did everything in two takes and after we mixed it, I said, 'We've got a smash here.'

"Then Epic released the record and it didn't do a thing. I mean absolutely nothing. Zero point zero. I finally said, 'That's it. I give up.'"

Everyone forgot about the record and went on to other projects. But then, about nine months later, Vance received a call from an Epic promotion man in Kansas who thought "Playground in My Mind" had a shot at making it on the charts. "He told me, 'I get so many releases, but my kid happened to pick this record up and play it and all his friends are saying how great it is. I think you've got a hit here. I'm taking it to the biggest station in Kansas.' The station played it and the phones started ringing off the wall. Soon the song spread throughout the midwest.

"Clive Davis, who was the head of Epic back then, got wind of what was happening and he put the promotion wheels in motion," said Vance. "And the rest is history. The song sold over two million records."

Most surprised of all was Clint Holmes. Talking to an interviewer years later, Holmes recalled, "I got a call from Epic telling me, 'Your record's gonna hit the Hot 100 this week, and it looks like it could make the Top 40.' I didn't even know what record he was talking about. I was amazed."

— PLATTER PATTER —

After "Playground in My Mind" fell off the charts, Clint Holmes refused to sing the song in his nightclub act.

"You know, in some sense, 'Playground' hurt me," he told a reporter in 1982. "It branded me as a novelty singer because I didn't follow it up with something more substantial. We recorded another song in a similar vein, which I did not want to do. It was called 'Shiddle-ee-Dee,' and the very title tells you what the song was like—a bomb."

Michael Ochs Archives

Only then did Holmes change his image back to a singer of more mature music. But he never made it back on the charts again.

Although "Playground" was a big hit, it wasn't a career-making record for him because, he said, "a lot of people remember the song but not the fellow who sang it."

— ROCK ON —

Clint Holmes still performs in nightclubs.

He was last seen on television in 1986-87 as the sidekick to comedienne Joan Rivers on her ill-fated "The Late Show" on the Fox Network.

Playground in My Mind

Ba ba ba ba ba
Ba ba ba ba ba
Ba ba ba ba ba
Ba ba ba ba.

Ba ba ba ba ba
Ba ba ba ba ba
Ba ba ba ba ba ba.

When this old world gets me down
And there's no love to be found
I close my eyes and soon I find
I'm in a playground in my mind

Where the children laugh
And the children play
And we sing a song all day

My name is Michael, I got a nickel
I got a nickel shiny and new
I'm gonna buy me all kinds of candy
That's what I'm gonna do

Oh, the wonders that I find
In the playground in my mind
In a world that used to be
Close your eyes and follow me

Where the children laugh
And the children play
And we sing a song all day

My girl is Cindy, when we get married
We're gonna have a baby or two
We're gonna let them visit their
  grandma
That's what we're gonna do

See the little children
Living in a world that I left behind
Happy little children
In the playground in my mind

See the little children
See how they play so happy
In the playground in my mind

BOHEMIAN RHAPSODY
Queen

#22

FOR THE RECORD

Released by Elektra in December, 1975.
Playing time: 5:52.
Topped the charts in England for nine weeks.
Climbed as high as #9 on the *Billboard* Hot 100 in the U.S. in 1976.
Was Queen's first million-selling single.
Became a hit again 16 years later, after being featured in the film *Wayne's World*.

BACKGROUND MUSIC

It was called an operatic mishmash, a bizarre opus, a mock opera. It featured a chorus wailing and chirping about "Scaramouch," "thunderbolt and lightning," "Beelzebub," "Galileo," and "Mama mia." And it drove its listeners to the record store . . . or to distraction.

"It" was the strange creation of Freddie Mercury, the outlandish lead singer of the British rock group Queen. "I always wanted to do something operatic," he once told reporters. "I don't really know anything about opera myself. It was as far as my limited capacity could take me."

"Bo Rap," as the song came to be called, was Queen's most talked-about tune. The band was formed in 1970 when all four members were students in London. They wrote and rehearsed their songs for three years before they felt ready to perform live. Meanwhile, they earned college degrees—Mercury in graphics and illustration, guitarist

Brian May in astronomy, bassist John Deacon in electronics, and drummer Roger Taylor in biology.

Queen became Britain's most glittering rock group by combining gaudy theatrical pomp with heavy metal bluster. In concerts, Mercury often appeared in leather storm-trooper outfits or women's clothes.

While Queen was working on their fourth album, producer Roy Thomas Baker recalled, "Freddie said he'd written this new song and sat at the piano and sang me bits of 'Bohemian Rhapsody.' Then he said, 'Now this is where the opera section comes in, dear,' and I fell down laughing." But Mercury was serious.

While recording the song, which was done in sections, the length of the operatic part kept increasing. "It was supposed to be five or ten seconds, but when we started the sessions, it went to a minute, then more," said Baker.

"Freddie would walk in and say,

'I've got some new ideas for the vocals. We'll stick some "Galileos" in here.' The middle section got longer and longer, so we kept adding bits of blank tape to it. We just went 'more, more, more' until the recording head on the tape machine literally broke off.

"It was a period of continual singing and laughing. It was so funny to do that we were all in hysterics while recording it."

Recalled guitarist Brian May, "We ran the tape through so many times it kept wearing out. Once we held the tape up to the light and we could see straight through it. The music had practically vanished. We transferred it in a hurry. Strange business—holding on to this elusive sound signal which gradually disappeared as we created it."

After the song was recorded, Baker recalled, Queen wanted it released as a single. "So we phoned up our English record company and I told them we had a single that was seven minutes long and they said it wouldn't get any airplay because it was too long. But I reminded them of 'Mac-Arthur Park' (see page 177) which was about the same length."

Queen then enlisted the help of London disc jockey Kenny Everett, who loved the song. They asked him not to play it on the radio—and then winked. So the next day, he told his radio listeners, "I've got the latest single here from Queen, but they told me strictly not to play it. Oh, my finger's slipped!" He played the song 14 times over the weekend, igniting a huge demand for the record from fans.

NOTEWORTHY NOTES

- The opera section in "Bo Rap" was done over seven 12-hour days of singing.

- The song features 180 vocal overdubs.

- The lyrics were so incomprehensible that a London radio station ran a competition which invited listeners to submit their interpretations of the story line.

- The song was edited from over seven minutes when it first aired down to 5:52 when it was pressed.

- The nine-week run of "Bo Rap" at the top of the British charts was the longest since Paul Anka's "Diana" in 1957.

PLATTER PATTER

The title of the album on which "Bohemian Rhapsody" is featured, "A Night at the Opera," was inspired by the zany Marx Brothers.

While working on the album, the members of Queen were bickering

Michael Ochs Archives

over creative differences when their producer, Roy Thomas Baker, invited them to his home for a break. "Nobody wanted to come to my house because they were all feeling miserable, but I said they should come and we could watch a movie and everyone could get drunk," Baker said.

So he played the Marx Brothers' 1935 film comedy *A Night at the Opera*. "It cheered everyone up," said Baker. "It was either Freddie or Roger Taylor who suggested that we call the album 'A Night at the Opera'—just as a joke. But I liked the idea because it sounded very funny, and that's how that record got its name—a combination of the fact that there was an opera section in the middle of 'Bohemian Rhapsody' and all of us watching the film."

FOLLOW UPS AND DOWNS

Queen followed up "Bo Rap" with the two-sided hit single "We Will Rock You/We Are the Champions" in 1977.

The next year, they came out with the notorious double single "Fat Bottomed Girls/Bicycle Race." It drew fire from feminists who objected to the title of the first song. There was even a bigger flap over the gatefold poster included in the LP, "Jazz," of 60 nude women at the start of a bicycle race that the band had staged in London.

To launch the album, Queen held its most outrageous party ever in New Orleans—a $200,000 tribute to debauchery. The bash featured topless waitresses, hermaphrodite strippers, dwarfs, and a woman who smoked cigarettes from an orifice that precluded any possible concerns about lung cancer.

In 1980, Queen scored #1 hits with "Crazy Little Thing Called Love" and "Another One Bites the Dust."

ROCK ON

After 20 years and album sales of nearly 90 million copies, the members of Queen began producing music on a solo basis after lead singer Freddie Mercury died in 1991 from pneumonia brought on by AIDS. He was 45 years old.

Mercury, whose real name was Frederick Bulsara, had not performed with Queen in concert since 1986. He had become a virtual recluse and repeatedly denied he had contracted AIDS until the day before his death.

"Freddie was clearly out in left field someplace, outrageous onstage and offstage," said Capitol-EMI president Joe Smith. "He was the band's driving force."

Bohemian Rhapsody

*Is this the real life
Is this just fantasy
Caught in a landslide
No escape from reality
Open your eyes
Look up to the skies and see
I'm just a poor boy
I need no sympathy
Because I'm easy come, easy go
A little high, little low
Anyway the wind blows
Doesn't really matter to me
To me.*

*Mama, just killed a man
Put a gun against his head
Pulled my trigger, now he's dead
Mama, life had just begun
But now I've gone and thrown it all
    away
Mama, ooh
Didn't mean to make you cry
If I'm not back again this time
    tomorrow
Carry on
Carry on
As if nothing really matters.*

*Too late, my time has come
Sends shivers down my spine
Body's aching all the time
Goodbye everybody, I've got to go
Gotta leave you all behind and face
    the truth*

*Mama, ooh
I don't want to die
I sometimes wish I'd never been born
    at all.*

*I see a little silhouetto of a man
Scaramouch, scaramouch
Will you do the Fandango
Thunderbolt and lightning, very, very
    frightening me
Galileo, Galileo
Galileo, Galileo
Galileo figaro, magnifico
But I'm just a poor boy and nobody
    loves me
He's just a poor boy from a poor
    family
Spare him his life from this monstrosity
Easy come, easy go, will you let me go
Bismillah!
No, we will not let you go, let him go
Bismillah!
We will not let you go, let him go
Bismillah!
We will not let you go, let me go
Will not let you go, let me go
Will not let you go, let me go
No, no, no, no, no, no, no
Mama mia, mama mia, mama mia let
    me go
Beelzebub has a devil put aside for me
For me, for me.*

*So you think you can stone me and
    spit in my eye*
*So you think you can love me and
    leave me to die*
Oh baby,
Can't do this to me baby
*Just gotta get out, just gotta get right
    outta here.*

Nothing really matters
Anyone can see
Nothing really matters
Nothing really matters to me.

Anyway the wind blows . . .

JUNK FOOD JUNKIE

Larry Groce

FOR THE RECORD

Released by Warner Brothers Records in 1976.
Playing time: 3:03.
Was Groce's only hit, making it as high as #9 on the *Billboard* Hot 100.

BACKGROUND MUSIC

This silly song about addiction to such goodies as corn chips, moon pies, and Twinkies was written and performed by a self-confessed junk food junkie.

"That's the way I always ate when I was a kid," admitted Larry Groce. "No matter how hard my mother tried, I ended up eating a peanut butter sandwich and Fritos and drinking Dr. Pepper. That was pretty much the staple."

Groce, who sang folk songs at coffeehouses, was eating junk food on the road when he conjured up the song in the mid 1970s. "I wrote it in my Volkswagen bus as I drove from West Virginia to Boston to do a job," he recalled. "I knew I wanted to write a song about junk food. So I got the idea to use the character of a junk food junkie who was kind of a Jekyll and Hyde. The words came fairly quickly. I actually stopped on the side of the road, took out the guitar, and made a tune for it so that by the time I got to Boston, it was pretty well written."

Groce sang the song in his act on the coffeehouse circuit and received a strong positive reaction. "I thought of 'Junk Food Junkie' more as a satire than a novelty song. I performed it to poke fun at both the junk food culture and the health food culture. Everybody identified with it."

His best reception came from the audience at a New York coffeehouse called The Focus, where he played regularly. "It turned into a health food restaurant. I saw the irony of going from the junk food culture of my childhood to the hip New York health conciousness where brown rice was the staple."

His manager, Randy Nauert, tried to secure a record deal. But when there were no takers, Nauert decided to put it out himself on his own label, Peaceable Records. He sent several hundred copies to radio stations around the country. "The song sold itself," said Groce. "Disc jockeys had so much fun with it that it took on a life of its own."

Dr. Demento featured it on his syndicated radio show, and in a weekly phone-in contest on Denver's KTLK,

"Junk Food Junkie" soundly trounced all comers. The song finally caught the attention of Warner Brothers, who cut a deal with Groce and re-released it on their label. Only then did it become a national hit.

NOTEWORTHY NOTES

- The song was recorded live at McCabe's—a Los Angeles guitar shop that still stages acoustic concerts right in the store.

- Groce didn't even realize that his song was being recorded for a single. "I wasn't aware they were recording it because at the time I hadn't planned on releasing it as a single," he said.

- The audience's applause was sweetened for the record, "but not too much," Groce said.

- Groce's was the first song in history with lyrics that mentioned both 19th century poet John Keats and Kentucky Fried Chicken founder Colonel Sanders.

- Michael Jackson once sang "Junk Food Junkie" on the Jackson Five's network TV show.

PLATTER PATTER

Warner Brothers Records feared there would be a costly backlash from the junk food companies who were mentioned by name in the song.

"There was a fear," said Groce. "I was in the publicity department at Warner Brothers and they were worried because they heard that local outlets of McDonald's and Kentucky Fried Chicken had put some heat on the local stations to drop the song from their playlists.

"Although there were a few local franchises who were upset with the song and thought it was an insult, the home offices understood that every time their name was mentioned good things happen."

After the song became a hit, Groce was a guest on a radio show along with the creator of Twinkies, who believed any kind of publicity was good publicity. "He said that every time Archie Bunker mentioned Twinkies on 'All in the Family'— whether he was making fun of them or not—sales went up," said Groce.

"We made a call to the P.R. office of Dr. Pepper and the guy there said they were in the company of some other good brand names [mentioned in the song] and they were happy about it."

Actually, Groce was a little disappointed that more companies weren't angry. "I was hoping someone would give us grief because that would have created a David and Goliath scenario that could have helped sales of the record. But I think most companies were smart enough to realize that poking fun at their product was in good fun.

"The Anti-Junk Food Council thought it was great because the song pointed out the dangers of junk food. I know a lot of people think junk food isn't nutritious—but I don't know anyone who doesn't agree that it tastes good."

FOLLOW UPS AND DOWNS

None of Groce's follow-up songs made it on the charts.

Among them were: "The Bumper Sticker Song," "We Been Malled," and "Turn on the TV."

ROCK ON

Larry Groce, who lives in a 120-year-old farmhouse in West Virginia, has recorded seven albums of his own folk songs and ballads as well as hymns. He's also made nine albums of children's songs for Walt Disney Records, five of which have gone gold and three platinum.

In 1986 he began hosting "Mountain Stage," a national radio show which features top recording artists from all styles of music. In 1991

PHOTO COURTESY: Steve Payne

Groce starred in a low-budget made-for-video feature film called *Paradise Park*. "It's a humorous story of a trailer park in West Virginia," said Groce. "I play a teacher who lives there and everyone is an oddball but me."

Junk Food Junkie

You know I love that organic cooking
I always ask for more
And they call me Mr. Natural
On down to the health food store
I only eat good sea salt
White sugar don't touch my lips
And my friends is always
Begging me to take them
On macrobiotic trips
Yes, they are

Oh, but at night I stake out my
    strongbox
That I keep under lock and key
And I take it off to my closet
Where nobody else can see
I open that door so slowly
Take a peek up north and south
Then I pull out a Hostess Twinkie
And I pop it in my mouth

Yeah, in the daytime I'm Mr. Natural
Just as healthy as I can be
But at night I'm a junk food junkie
Good lord have pity on me

Well, at lunchtime
You can always find me
At the Whole Earth Vitamin Bar
Just sucking on my plain white yogurt
From my hand thrown pottery jar
And sippin' a little hand pressed cider
With a carrot stick for desert
And wiping my face
In a natural way
On the sleeve of my peasant shirt
Oh yeah

Ah, but when that clock strikes
    midnight

And I'm all by myself
I work that combination
On my secret hideaway shelf
And I pull out some Fritos corn chips
Dr. Pepper and an Ole Moon Pie
Then I sit back in glorious expectation
Of a genuine junk food high

Oh yeah, in the daytime I'm Mr.
    Natural
Just as healthy as I can be
But at night I'm a junk food junkie
Good lord have pity on me

My friends down at the commune
They think I'm pretty neat
Oh, I don't know nothing about arts
    and crafts
But I give 'em all something to eat
I'm a friend to old Euell Gibbons
And I only eat homegrown spice
I got a John Keats
Autographed Grecian urn
Filled up with my brown rice
Yes, I do

Oh, but folks lately I have been spotted
With a Big Mac on my breath
Stumbling into a Colonel Sanders
With a face as white as death
I'm afraid someday they'll find me
Just stretched out on my bed
With a handful of Pringles Potato
    Chips
And a Ding Dong by my head

In the daytime I'm Mr. Natural
Just as healthy as I can be
But at night I'm a junk food junkie
Good lord have pity on me

THE HOMECOMING QUEEN'S GOT A GUN

Julie Brown

#20

FOR THE RECORD

Released independently by Julie Brown in 1984.
Playing time: 4:36.
Sold 20,000 copies.
Included in the EP "Goddess in Progress" released by Rhino Records in 1985;
and, later, on the Sire Records album "Trapped in the Body of a White Girl."

BACKGROUND MUSIC

Art imitates life department: Pop jester Julie Brown created this cult classic of a crazed murder-mad coed because she herself had lost out in her high school's homecoming queen contest.

"I was a homecoming princess, not the queen," recalled Julie of her one big disappointment at Van Nuys High in California. "I think the queen totally manipulated people to get the title. Not to be vicious or anything, but she wasn't as popular as she should have been to get that title.

"I was bitter because I wasn't the queen. I think that's why the song popped up from my unconscious."

After recovering emotionally from that high school setback, Brown, an honor student, enrolled at California State University at Northridge to study anthropology. "That lasted about a minute," she said. "I thought we'd be going on digs, but you had to read textbooks and learn chemistry."

Julie then studied drama at Valley Junior College before joining the stuffy American Conservatory Theater in San Francisco. "I was very serious about doing theater," she said. "But after a while, I just started goofing around. I felt compelled to make jokes."

With partner Charlie Coffey, Julie wrote and performed in a review called "Atomic Comedy." The duo played in area clubs and opened for such stars as Robin Williams. "It was the first time I started using music in my comedy act," she said. "I played Anita Bryant and did a song called 'Don't Make My Child a Homo' and 'Love from the Waist Up.'"

Julie eventually went solo as a

stand-up comedian in Los Angeles where she also made appearances on TV sitcoms such as "The Jeffersons," "Happy Days," "Laverne & Shirley," and "Newhart."

"I got sick of doing stand-up," she said. "You've got to be such a tough cookie and pretend that your feelings don't get hurt when they don't laugh. I played so many bad places. I actually performed on a pool table because there was no stage. They had to build stairs for me out of old beer boxes so I could get onto the pool table. The microphone was hooked to a wire coming out of the ceiling. I was ready for a change."

When Frank and Moon Unit Zappa's wacky tune, "Valley Girl," became a hit, Julie was inspired to redirect her career. "I was doing a Valley Girl character in my act, so when the song came out, I was real depressed," Julie said. "Everyone was telling me, 'You should have done that song.' Then I thought, 'Why can't I do records?' So I started writing songs, working with musicians, and taking voice lessons.

"One day I was driving on the freeway and this title just came to me: 'The Homecoming Queen's Got a Gun.' And I knew immediately what it was going to be about." Julie and Charlie Coffey conjured up a perfect blonde queen who guns down nearly everyone at the prom while her best friend shouts in typical Valley Girl logic: "Stop it, Debbie, you're embarrassing me!"

Julie also wrote "I Like 'Em Big and Stupid"—an ode to a woman's guiltless, mindless sex with a hunk: "I go bar hopping and they say last call/I start shopping for a Neanderthal . . . Smart guys are nowhere—they make demands/Give me a moron with talented hands."

Actor Terrence McNally, Julie's husband-to-be, loved the songs so much he offered to produce them himself. With "I Like 'Em Big and Stupid" on the flip side, 20,000 copies of "The Homecoming Queen's Got a Gun" were pressed. After free records were sent to hip DJs and college radio stations around the country, the song began to get wide airplay.

Meanwhile, Julie made her own video of the song that brought Debbie's murderous saga—and her cartoonishly bloodless killings—to life. The singer played both the pistol-packing prom queen and her embarrassed best friend. However, MTV, apparently unfamiliar with the idea of satire, deemed the video too violent for the tender sensibilities of its viewers. "It's really absurd," said Julie at the time. "The video is as violent as a Roadrunner cartoon."

Undaunted, Julie and her fiance sold all 20,000 copies of the record out of their house. "It was really a nightmare trying to collect from independent distributors, doing phone interviews, and turning our home into a record warehouse," she said. Eventually, the couple made a deal with Rhino Records to include the two songs with three others on an EP called "Goddess in Progress." It became one of Rhino's biggest sellers.

— NOTEWORTHY NOTES —

Julie and her writing partner, Charlie Coffey, wrote 14 drafts of "The Homecoming Queen's Got a Gun."

"There were other characters who got killed off and other incidents in earlier versions," said Brown. "But the song was getting too long, so we took only the best verses.

"We had a good time writing it. We laughed a lot."

—— PLATTER PATTER ——

The first time Julie Brown sang "The Homecoming Queen's Got a Gun" live, it bombed—because she performed it at a bar mitzvah!

"I had just recorded the song in the studio and I thought, 'I've got to try this out live,'" she recalled. "Budd Friedman, who runs the Improv, had booked a bar mitzvah during the day and asked me to sing.

"I was so excited about this new song that I sang 'The Homecoming Queen's Got a Gun' at the bar mitzvah.

Alberto Tolot

I don't know what I was thinking about. I remember that as I was singing, the mothers were staring at me like I was out of my mind. I realized then it was just so wrong, but I went ahead and sang it. That was not a good choice."

———— ROCK ON ————

Julie co-wrote the screenplay to the movie *Earth Girls Are Easy* in which she also co-starred with Geena Davis. Julie, who co-starred in the Fox network's comedy show "The Edge," continues to pursue an acting career.

The Homecoming Queen's Got a Gun

It was homecoming night at my high
school
Everyone was there, it was totally cool
I was really excited, I almost wet my
jeans
'Cause my best friend Debbie was
Homecoming Queen

She looked so pretty in pink chiffon
Riding the float with her tiara on
Holding this humongous bouquet in
her hand
She looked straight out of Disneyland
You know, like the Cinderella ride
I mean definitely an E ticket

The crowd was cheering
Everyone was stoked
I mean it was like the whole school
Was totally coked or something
The band was playing "Evergreen"
When all of a sudden somebody
screamed
"Look out! The Homecoming Queen's
got a gun!"

Everybody run
The Homecoming Queen's got a gun
Everybody run
The Homecoming Queen has got a gun

Debbie's smiling and waving her gun
Picking off cheerleaders one by one
Oh, Buffy's pom-pom just blew to bits
Oh no, Mitzi's head just did the splits
God, my best friend's on a shooting
spree
Stop it, Debbie, you're embarrassing me
How could you do what you just did?
Are you having a really bad period?

Everybody run
The Homecoming Queen's got a gun
Everybody run
The Homecoming Queen has got a gun

An hour later the cops arrived
By then the entire glee club had died
You wouldn't believe what they
brought to stop her
Tear gas, machine guns, even a
chopper.

"Throw down your gun and tiara
and come out of the float!"
Debbie didn't listen to what the cop
said
She aimed and fired and now the math
teacher's dead
Its really sad, but kind of a relief
I mean, we had this big test coming up
next week

Everybody run
The Homecoming Queen's got a gun
Everybody run
The Homecoming Queen has got a gun

The cops fired a warning shot that
blew her off the float
I tried to scream "Duck," but it stuck
in my throat
She hit the ground and did a flip
It was real acrobatic
But I was crying so hard, I couldn't
work my instamatic

I ran down to Debbie
I had to find out
What made her do it
Why'd she freak out
I saw the bullet had got her right in
    the ear
I knew then the end was near

So I ran down
And I said in her good ear
"Debbie, why'd you do it?"
She raised her head, smiled, and said
"I did it for Johnny!"

Johnny? Well, like who's Johnny?
Answer me, Debbie. Who's Johnny?
Does anybody here know Johnny?

Are you Johnny?
There was one guy named Johnny,
But he was a total geek
He always had food in his braces
Answer me, Debbie. Who's Johnny?
Oh God, that is like that movie Citizen
    Kane
You know, where you later find out
    "Rosebud" was a sled
But we'll never know who Johnny was
'Cause, like, she's dead

Everybody run
The Homecoming Queen's got a gun
Everybody run
The Homecoming Queen has got a gun

MR. CUSTER

Larry Verne

#19

―――――――― FOR THE RECORD ――――――――

Released by Era Records in 1960.
Playing time: 2:59.
Climbed to #1 on the *Billboard* Hot 100 and stayed there for a week.

――――――――――― BACKGROUND MUSIC ―――――――――――

If ever there was a record that had a lot going against it, "Mr. Custer" was the one. The songwriting team was still scrambling to finish the tune at the recording session, the lead singer had no musical experience (or talent, for that matter), and the song poked fun at the massacre of hundreds of U.S. soldiers.

It didn't seem possible that such a record could ever be released, let alone become a number one hit. Yet that's exactly what happened to this spoof of General George Custer's fatal encounter at Little Big Horn.

In the late 1950s, Fred Darian, a singer from Detroit, and Joe Van Winkle, who yearned to write songs but couldn't read music, teamed up with composer Al DeLory. Although their music was serious, they were always laughing it up. Somehow, they found humor in Custer's ill-fated decision to attack Chief Sitting Bull. (The general and all 254 of his U.S. cavalry troops were killed at Little Big Horn in 1876.)

"'Mr. Custer' was not a song that we just sat down and wrote," said

Darian. "It just developed as we went along. One day we were joking around when Al came up with the line, 'Mr. Custer, I don't want to go.' And then somebody said, 'Forward, ho!' And then somebody else made a sound like an arrow. We rolled over from laughter and slapped each other on the back and said, 'Isn't that funny?'"

After the writing team developed a vague outline, they decided to make a demo of the song. There was only one problem. They needed the right kind of singer to pull it off. "We had no one to sing the lead," said Van Winkle. "Here we were in our small $40-a-month office, which was nothing more than a room with a piano, wondering who we could get to be the lead voice."

So they turned to Larry Verne, an acquaintance who had never sung professionally in his life.

Verne, who once admitted he "wasn't serious about nothin'," had drifted from job to job as a truck driver, bartender, TV stunt man, and a photographer's assistant. "The photo studio was right across the hall [from the songwriting team] so I got to know them at the time they were writing 'Mr. Custer,'" Verne recalled.

The trio often invited Verne to schmooz with them over coffee. "He was kind of a refreshing country boy who spoke with a drawl," said Darian. "So we asked him to come in and do a demo for us. We didn't know if he could sing or not. But our song didn't take a real singer. It took an actor."

Said Verne, "They invited me to the recording studio to make a demo of the song. When I got there, they said, 'Okay, Larry, you go in the booth and do it.'"

Although they had found their lead singer, the trio was faced with another problem: the song wasn't completely written. "We had the story line and some key phrases," said Darian. "So we kept on writing right in the studio. It was fun. Joe, Al, and I did the chorus and all the Indian sounds in the background and the 'Forward, ho!'"

Then they took the song to every major record company—and were promptly shot down. "We hit the independents next and met the same fate," said Van Winkle.

The never-say-die trio next took the record to Bob Keene, of Del-Fi Records, which had released Richie Valens' "La Bamba." He thought "Mr. Custer" was an "interesting" song, gave the group a $300 advance, and said he'd try to get it released. "We kept waiting and waiting and trying to get him to put the record out," said Darian. "Finally, after several months, we called him and asked, 'When's the

record coming out?' And he said, 'You know, I don't think it's so funny anymore.'"

The persevering trio decided to make another demo of "Mr. Custer" because the first one had all but been worn out. While they were making a new recording at Gold Star Studio, Herb Newman of Era Records was in the hallway and heard the song. Recalled Van Winkle, "He came in and said, 'That's kind of funny. Do you want me to put it out?' We said, 'Yes, of course!'"

Era Records released "Mr. Custer"—and it catapulted to the top. "Bob Keene wanted to kill himself," said Van Winkle. "Meanwhile, Herb Newman was turning white because nothing like this had ever happened to him before. He was getting 40,000 record orders a day.

"Everybody was in shock. Keep in mind that for months and months, we had been told, 'It's a bomb,' 'Nobody wants it,' and 'You're fooling yourselves.'"

They called Larry with the good news: "Larry, you've got a hit record!" Then they put him on tour. "We took Larry back east and did some crazy things," said Van Winkle.

"In Philadelphia, for example, we had him dressed up in a cavalry uniform directing traffic. He was willing to do anything for a laugh. And wherever he went, sales of the record skyrocketed.

"I've often thought about why the song was a hit. We all know what happened to Mr. Custer. So when you hear this pathetic little voice saying he doesn't want to go, it's funny. We turned tragedy into humor."

— PLATTER PATTER —

While searching for an independent record company willing to release "Mr. Custer," the songwriting team hit rock bottom.

"The crowning disappointment was when we went into a dingy storefront record company that had no furniture except a little record player on a table," recalled Joe Van Winkle. "This old woman and younger man listened to 'Mr. Custer.' They never smiled and never said a word until it was over. Then the

PHOTO COURTESY: Fred Bronson

woman gave us the record back and said, 'That's the most horrible thing I ever heard in my life! All those people got killed. No one will buy it because it's a horrible record!'"

FOLLOW UPS AND DOWNS

Larry Verne followed up "Mr. Custer" with "Mister Livingston," a spoof on Stanley's hunt for Livingston in Africa. The record peaked at #75. Among other later songs that bombed were "Abdul's Party" and "The Porcupine Patrol."

ROCK ON

When the follow-up records flopped, Larry Verne gave up music and became a construction foreman for a movie studio and an assistant set director.

Joe Van Winkle left the music business a short while later and became a television producer and screenwriter.

Fred Darian produced Dobie Gray's 1965 hit "The In Crowd" and then became a singer on the nightclub circuit.

In 1970, Darian started a new career as a real estate agent.

MR. CUSTER   111

Mr. Custer

That famous day in history
The men of the Seventh Calvary
Went riding on.

And from the rear, a voice was heard
A brave young man with a trembling
   word
Rang loud and clear
What am I doing here?

Please Mr. Custer
I don't want to go
Hey Mr. Custer
Please don't make me go.

I had a dream last night
About the coming fight
Somebody yelled attack
And there I stood
With an arrow in my back.

Please Mr. Custer
I don't want to go
Forward ho
No.

Look at them bushes out there
They movin'
There's an injun behind every one
Hey Mr. Custer
You mind if I be excused
The rest of the afternoon?
Hey Charlie, duck your head
Well, you're a little bit late on that
   one, Charlie
Ooh, I bet that smarts

They were sure of victory
The men of the Seventh Cavalry
As they rode on.

But again from the rear, a voice was
   heard
That same brave voice with a
   trembling word
Rang loud and clear
What am I doing here?

Please Mr. Custer
I don't want to go
Hey Mr. Custer
Please don't make me go.

There's a redskin waiting out there
He's fixing to take my hair
A coward I've been called
'Cause I don't want to wind up
Dead or bald.

Please Mr. Custer
I don't want to go
Forward ho
No.

I wonder what the injun word for
   friend is
Let's see, friend
Kemo sabe, that's it. Kemo sabe
Hey out there, kemo sabe
Well, that isn't it
Look at them
Out running around like a bunch of
   wild injuns
Ha, ha, ha
Oh, this ain't no time for joking.

SURFIN' BIRD

The Trashmen

FOR THE RECORD

Released by Garrett Records in 1963.
Playing time: 2:20.
Peaked at #4 on the *Billboard* Hot 100 in 1964.

BACKGROUND MUSIC

In a cruel twist of fate, one singing group recorded two songs that had only modest success—only to see another band combine the tunes into a smash hit record.

In 1960, four young men fresh out of high school in Minneapolis—Dal Winslow, Steve Wahrer, Tony Andreason, and Bob Reed—formed a band that played at local dances. "We did your standard rock and roll sets that everybody else was doing," Winslow recalled.

"Then we decided to change our style. We wanted to become a surf band. So we went to California, heard the surf bands, and bought tons of surf albums. We came back home and locked ourselves away and started practicing. We had played under several names in the past, and we now called ourselves the Trashmen. Then we began performing again and the kids went bananas. They loved us."

Meanwhile, in California, a backup group who often sang under such names as The Sharps, The Four After Fives, and The Crenshaws, had been busy cutting records that never seemed to sell. One day during rehearsal, group member Rocky Wilson began singing, "Papa-oom-mow-mow" as a joke, recalled singer Al Frazier. "We all cracked up. Then [member] Carl White said, 'Hell, that's the funniest thing I ever heard, man! You can't understand a word he's saying.' We talked about it and laughed and kicked it back and forth. About ten hours later, we had the song on tape. We're all credited with writing it. My input was 'dit-dit-dit.'

"I played it for Jack Levy and Adam Ross at Pan-or Productions and they started turning cartwheels in the room. Jack said, 'This is fantastic! I've got to have it. I'm gonna give you a check for $1,200 and then we'll talk about more money later.' I almost fainted. I said, 'Twelve hundred dollars—in one check?' We never saw that kind of money before."

Levy and Ross decided to change the group's name to the Rivingtons because the two producers once lived on Rivington Street in New York. Then they had the group record the song—"Papa-Oom-Mow-Mow"—that very night. Capitol Records turned it down because it was "too wild" for them, but Liberty Records agreed to distribute it. "Unfortunately," said Frazier, "they didn't know how to handle it." Although it was a hit in California, the record made it only up to #48 on the *Billboard* Hot 100.

Because kids were dancing The Bird—the latest craze at the time—to "Papa-Oom-Mow-Mow," the Rivingtons quickly followed up with a new record called "The Bird's The Word." But like "Papa-Oom-Mow-Mow," the record stalled after climbing halfway up the charts.

Back in the midwest, the Trashmen heard a group in a Wisconsin bar play its own version of a medley of "Papa-Oom-Mow-Mow" and "The Bird's The Word." Recalled Dal Winslow, "We decided that's something we'll do onstage as kind of a novelty. Since we didn't know the words, we kind of improvised, and that's how 'Surfin' Bird' was born.

"We didn't know that the Rivingtons had recorded 'The Bird's The Word' or 'Papa-Oom-Mow-Mow.' We just threw our own thing together after hearing that medley one night in a bar. At the dances we were playing at, the response was overwhelming. So we cut a record and it just took off."

NOTEWORTHY NOTES

- The Trashmen first recorded "Surfin' Bird" in the basement studio of the Garrett Record Store in Minneapolis. But when a disc jockey told them the record needed to be polished before he would play it, they re-recorded it at a studio that cut radio commercials.

- "Surfin' Bird" was sung by drummer Steve Wahrer, who appeared alone on Dick Clark's American Bandstand. "Clark was just moving from Philadelphia to California so all he could afford was travel expenses for one person," recalled Winslow. "We didn't have the money, so we sent Steve."

PLATTER PATTER

The Trashmen used to be known as the Citations, but when they changed their image from strictly a rock and roll band to a surf band, they wanted a new name.

"We went through a bunch of records, looking for ideas for a name," said Winslow. "We found a locally-produced record called 'The Trashman's Blues' and we said, 'Let's call ourselves the Trashmen. At least people will remember our name.'

"We had trouble back then in some towns getting our name publicized because people thought the Trashmen meant something bad."

Michael Ochs Archives

FOLLOW UPS AND DOWNS

The Trashmen followed up "Surfin' Bird" with "Bird Dance Beat," which reached #30 in 1964. "It was written by George Garrett, who owned the record store where we first recorded," said Winslow. "We needed a follow-up record right away in the same mold. But by then, the timing was wrong because the British invasion was well upon us."

ROCK ON

Dal Winslow is in charge of telecommunications and planning and design for a bank corporation in Minnesota.

Bass player Bob Reed is the manager of a tool and die company. Guitarist Tony Andreason deals with securities and annuities. Drummer Steve Wahrer, who sang "Surfin' Bird," died of throat cancer.

"In our spare time, we still play various parks in the summer and rock and roll shows," said Winslow. "Tony's brother Mark fills in on the drums."

SURFIN' BIRD   115

Surfin' Bird

Well everybody's heard about the bird
Bird, bird, bird, bird's the word
Well bird, bird, bird is the word
Well bird, bird, well the bird is the
    word
Well bird, bird, bird's the word
Well bird, bird, well the bird is the
    word
Well bird, bird, bird's the word
Well bird, bird, bird, bird's the word
Well bird, bird, bird, well the bird is
    the word
Well bird, bird, bird, bird's the word
Well don't you know about the bird
Well everybody knows that the bird is
    the word
Well bird, bird, bird, the bird
Well . . .

Well everybody's heard about the bird
Well bird, bird, bird's the word
Well bird, bird, bird, bird's the word
Well bird, bird, bird, bird's the word
Well bird, bird, bird's the word
Well bird, bird, bird, bird's the word
Well bird, bird, bird, bird's the word
Well bird, bird, bird, bird's the word
Well bird, bird, bird, bird's the word
Well don't you know about the bird
Well everybody's talking about the bird
Well bird, bird, bird, bird
Well the bird
Surfin' bird . . .

Papa papa papa papa papa papa
    papa papa
Papa oom mow mow, papa oom mow
    mow mow
Papa oom mow mow, papa oom mow
    mow mow
Papa mow mow mow, papa oom mow
    mow
Papa oom mow mow, papa oom mow
    mow mow
Papa oom mow mow, papa mow mow
Oom ma ma ma ma mow mow, papa
    mow mow mow
Papa papa mow mow mow
Papa oom mow mow mow, oom mow
    mow mow
Papa mow mow mow, papa oom mow
    mow mow
Papa oom mow mow, papa oom mow
    mow mow
Oom mow mow mow, papa oom mow
    mow mow
Oom mow mow mow, papa papa mow
    mow mow
Papa mow mow mow, oom mow mow
    mow
Papa oom mow mow mow, papa mow
    mow
Mow mow mow mow mow
Well don't you know about the bird
Well everybody knows that the bird is
    the word
Well bird, bird, bird is the word.

CONVOY
C.W. McCall

#17

Released by MGM Records in 1975.
Playing time: 3:48.
Zoomed to #1 on the *Billboard* country chart in three weeks.
Climbed to #1 on the *Billboard* Hot 100 and stayed there for one week in 1976.
Became a gold single.

BACKGROUND MUSIC

This trucker's fantasy about a 1,000-truck convoy running amok, smashing through tollgates, ignoring cops, and taking the open road was created by an adman enthralled with the CB craze.

In the mid 1970s, Bill Fries (aka C.W. McCall) was a middle-aged art director for Bozell & Jacobs, an Omaha advertising agency. In his spare time, he liked to drive around the country, so he installed a CB in his jeep and got caught up in the CB mania that was sweeping America back then. His handle, or name on the air, was "Rubber Duck," and his wife's was "Smart Cookie." Whether he was on a weekend trip or going to and from work, Fries was always talking big rig lingo on his radio. He was "checking the seat covers" (watching out for a female driver with her skirt hiked high) while "keeping my nose between the ditches and Smokey out of my britches" (driving safely and looking out for speed traps). He soon developed an affinity for truckers.

From his office, which had a commanding view of Interstate 680, Fries thought the time was right to cash in the popularity of truckers, which had, after all, been triggered by the CB phenomenon. So for his client, Omaha's Metz Baking Company and its Old Home Bread, he dreamed up an ad campaign about a trucker. In the ads, a trucker named C.W. McCall would deliver a batch of Old Home Bread to the Old Home Filler-Up an' Keep on-a Truckin' Cafe where he would flirt with a waitress named Mavis. The radio spots sold a lot of bread and won a national award.

In the spring of 1974, following the advice of Sound Recorders president Don Sears, Fries spun off the Old Home commercials into a country single. Three weeks after its release, "Old Home Filler-Up an' Keep on-a Truckin' Cafe" had sold 30,000 copies locally. It eventually sold 100,000 copies nationwide and reached #54 on the country charts. Because of its success, Fries signed a five-year recording contract with MGM Records.

He recorded more offbeat trucking story songs like "Wolf Creek Pass," about a truck that loses its brakes while going over the Rockies, and "Classified," about the trials and tribulations of buying a used '57 pickup.

Although the songs performed well on the country charts, Fries was still a man in search of a big hit. He found it one day in 1975 when he conjured up "Convoy." While motoring down the interstate in his jeep and listening to his CB, Fries was the "back door," or last in a string of trucks and cars in contact with each other. "That's when I got the idea for 'Convoy,'" he said. "When I got home that night, I put the lyrics down and built the story into a fantasy of truckers in a convoy gaining power across the U.S. until they had an army of 1,000 trucks."

Fries liked the song so much that he tried to convince MGM to release it as a single. "They didn't want to do it," he recalled. "They said, 'Are you sure anyone out there will understand that CB garbage?'" As a result, MGM put "Convoy" on Fries' next country album, "Black Bear Road." But a few disc jockeys picked "Convoy" out of the album and played it. The switchboard lit up with requests to play the record again and again. Within days, MGM realized the song could be a monster hit and released it as a single.

"We hit a national nerve," said Fries. "Truckers have become cowboys to the American public." That's a big 10-4.

NOTEWORTHY NOTES

- Fries said the name he sang under, C.W. McCall, was a real person—a former trucker from Missouri with one arm.

- The song was such a huge hit that MGM had to put four record pressing plants in operation 24 hours a day to meet the demand.

- Fries wrote the lyrics, but the music was composed by Julliard-trained Chip Davis, one of his advertising associates.

PLATTER PATTER

Because they felt "Convoy" glorified highway lawlessness, various government officials condemned the record—and even tried to get it banned.

In Fries' home state of Iowa, the governor personally blasted the song's anti-cop attitude and pressured Des Moines' biggest radio station, WHO, to keep "Convoy" off the air. At first, the station complied, but it later put the record on its playlist.

Meanwhile, the FCC considered a plan to dispatch investigators to Atlanta to round up unlicensed CBers who were gathering to join Fries in a convoy for a radio station promotion.

"There were 1,200 vehicles on the interstate," Fries recalled. "There were bears in the air [helicopters] and smokeys [cops] everywhere. The idea was for each CBer to modulate [talk] with Rubber Duck for one minute." But the airwaves convulsed into chaos because everyone tried to talk at once.

Knowing that most CBers hadn't bothered to pay the $4 fee for a license, the FCC considered arresting everyone who didn't have a CB license at the promotion. But instead, the agency decided to play it cool and set up information booths to license the local CBers.

Amazed by the criticism from government officials, Fries said, "'Convoy' was more fun and games than a serious call to rise up and smash the tollgate."

FOLLOW UPS AND DOWNS

Under his alter ego C.W. McCall, Bill Fries followed up his hit with "There Won't Be No Country Music (There Won't Be No Rock 'N' Roll)" in 1976. He could have called it "There Won't Be No Follow-Up Hit," as the record only made it to #73.

ROCK ON

Despite his moderately successful early country songs and his one smash hit, Fries continued to work at the advertising agency for several years.

"Having all the stardom heaped on me, I didn't know how to react," he said.

Fries eventually retired and moved to a small town in Colorado to pursue other creative interests.

Michael Ochs Archives

C.W. McCall

Convoy

Yeah, breaker 1-9
This here's the Rubber Duck
You got a copy on me
Big Ben come on.

Yeah, 10-4 Big Ben
For sure, for sure
By golly, it's clean clear to Flagtown
Come on.

Yeah, it's a big 10-4 there, Big Ben
Yeah, we definitely got the front door,
    good buddy
Mercy sakes alive
It looks like we've got us a convoy.

It was the dark of the moon
On the sixth of June
In a Kenworth hauling logs
A cab over pete with a reefer on
And a jimmy hauling hogs.

We was heading for bear on I-10
About a mile out of Shakytown
I says, "Big Ben, this here's the
    Rubber Duck
And I'm about to put the hammer
    down."

'Cause we've got a little convoy
Rocking through the night
Yeah, we got a little convoy
Ain't she a beautiful sight
Come on and join our convoy
Ain't nothing gonna get in our way
We gonna roll this trucking convoy
Across the U.S.A.

Yeah, breaker Big Ben
This here's the Duck
And you wanna back off of them hogs
10-4, about five miles or so
10 roger, them hogs is getting intense
up here.

By the time we got into Tulsatown
We have 85 trucks in all
But there was a roadblock up on the
    cloverleaf
And them bears was wall to wall

Yeah, them smokies as thick as bugs
    on the bumper
They even had a bear in the air
I says, "Calling all trucks, this here's
    the Duck
We about to go a 'hunting bear.'

'Cause we've got a great big convoy
Rocking through the night
Yeah, we got a great big convoy
Ain't she a beautiful sight
Come on and join our convoy
Ain't nothing gonna get in our way
We gonna roll this trucking convoy
Across the U.S.A.

You wanna give me a 10-9 on that,
    Big Ben
Negatory, Big Ben. You're still too
    close.
Yeah, them hogs is starting to close up
    my sinuses.
Mercy sakes, you better back off
    another ten.

Well, we rolled up Interstate 44
Like a rocket sled on rails
We tore up all of our swindle sheets
And left 'em sittin' on the scales.

By the time we hit that Chi-town
Them bears was a 'getting' smart
They brought up some reinforcements
From the Illinois National Guard.

There's armored cars and tanks and
    jeeps
And rigs of every size
Yeah, them chicken coops was full of
    bears
And choppers filled the skies.

Well, we shot the line, we went for
    broke
With a thousand screaming trucks
And eleven long-haired Friends of
    Jesus
In a chartreuse microbus.

Yeah, Rubber Duck to Sodbuster, come
    on her
Yeah, 10-4 Sodbuster
Listen, you wanna put that microbus
Behind that suicide jockey
Yeah, he's hauling dynamite
And he needs all the help he can get.

Well, we laid a strip for the Jersey
    shore

Prepared to cross the line
I could see the bridge was lined with
    bears
But I didn't have a doggoned dime.

I says, "Big Ben, this here's the
    Rubber Duck
We just ain't a 'gonna pay no toll"
So we crashed the gate doing 98
I says, "Let them truckers roll, 10-4."

'Cause we've got a mighty convoy
Rocking through the night
Yeah, we got a mighty convoy
Ain't she a beautiful sight
Come on and join our convoy
Ain't nothing gonna get in our way
We gonna roll this trucking convoy
Across the U.S.A.

10-4 Big Ben, what's your 20?
Omaha? Well, they oughta know
What to do with those hogs out there
    for sure
Well, mercy sakes, good buddy
We gonna back on outta here
So keep the bugs off your glass
And the bears off your tail
We'll catch you on the flip-flop
This here's the Rubber Duck on the
    side
We gone, bye-bye.

ALLEY OOP

Hollywood Argyles

FOR THE RECORD

Released by Lute Records in 1960.
Playing time: 2:36.
Soared to #1 on the *Billboard* Hot 100, staying on top for one week.

BACKGROUND MUSIC

This goofy song about a prehistoric comic strip character was sung by a vocalist who had to form the Hollywood Argyles, a fake group, in order to avoid a lawsuit. It was the Argyles' only hit.

The group was the creation of Gary Paxton, who had always dreamed of making a hit record. A few years before "Alley Oop," Paxton and college buddy Clyde Battin teamed up in Phoenix to form the pop duo Skip and Flip. (Paxton was Flip.) They recorded a song called "It Was I" in 1959, which was released by Brent Records in Los Angeles. To the duo's pleasant surprise, the record climbed all the way to #11 on the *Billboard* Hot 100. Skip and Flip then went on a national tour, and Brent released another one of their tunes, "Fancy Nancy," but that only reached #71 on the charts.

The following year, Battin and Paxton broke up due to personal differences. But Paxton kept the duo alive by bringing in a new Skip—Dave Martinez, a former dishwasher from Phoenix, who was in turn eventually replaced by Rod Marshall. The revised Skip and Flip scored with "Cherry Pie," which climbed to #11 in 1960.

Then Paxton struck out on his own and headed for Hollywood to try his luck. "I was going down the freeway and I didn't know where Hollywood was," Paxton recalled. "I pulled off into an all-night filling station in Burbank at three in the morning. There were two attendants sitting on the top of a desk inside playing guitars. I asked, 'How do I get to Hollywood?' They drew me a map and we started talking and they recognized me from my Skip and Flip days. It turned out that the attendants—Dallas Frazier and Buddy Mize—wrote a lot of songs together, none of which had been recorded. So Dallas said, 'Let me sing you one,' and he sang 'Alley Oop.'"

The tune was about the comic strip character Alley Oop, the uncivilized, invincible caveman who battled the evil forces in the Kingdom of Moo and protected his sweetheart Oola. Eventually, in the strip, Alley and Oola were transported by a time machine to the 20th century where they faced a series of screwball adventures.

"I really liked the song and I told Dallas and Buddy that when I got settled, I would help produce it," Paxton said. "I drove on to Hollywood where I got a room at a flop house at the corner of El Centro and Selma for $7.50 a week. [Record producer] Kim Fowley lived there and we hooked up as business partners."

Paxton and Fowley formed a seat-of-the-pants music publishing company called Maverick Music. But since they were always short of cash, their office became Happy's Chevron service station. "We put a piece of plywood down on the grease bay and played guitars and wrote songs," Paxton recalled. "We used the pay phone there as our business number."

When they recorded "Alley Oop," Paxton hired several musicians to play in the session. Paxton, his girlfriend Diane, Frazier, and Mize sang the background while Sandy Nelson (who had a #4 hit a year earlier with "Teen Beat") played the garbage can and did the distinctive screaming.

"We started cutting the record at eight at night and didn't finish until six the next morning," Paxton said. "As we staggered outside the studio, I said, 'Hey, I'm still under contract to Skip and Flip. I can't use my name on this thing. What will we do?' The studio was right off Argyle Avenue so I said, 'We're in Hollywood and that's Argyle over there, so let's call ourselves the Hollywood Argyles.'

"I absolutely knew it was going to be a hit," he added.

The public loved the record, and it rose all the way to #1.

While he was settling his contract problem, Paxton needed the group to go on a national tour to promote the single. So he rounded up musicians from around the Los Angeles area and, while he stayed home, sent over a dozen groups—all claiming to be the Hollywood Argyles—out on the road!

PLATTER PATTER

Three different groups made the charts singing "Alley Oop"—all in the same year.

Although the Hollywood Argyles came out first with the song and saw it top the charts in 1960, they couldn't find a distributor for the record in New York.

So Larry Uttal, president of the Manhattan-based Madison Records, released a version of "Alley Oop" by Dante and the Evergreens which made it to #15. The version was produced by two struggling unknowns at the time, Herb Alpert and Lou Adler. (Both went on to fame and fortune, Alpert as a musician and founder of A&M Records and Adler as head of Ode Records.)

Despite—or maybe because of—the success of both records, a third group, the Dyna-Sores, put out their own version of "Alley Oop" later that same year, but it only reached as high as #59.

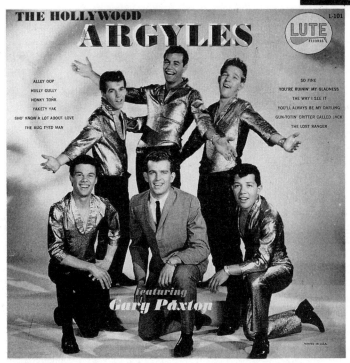

THE HOLLYWOOD ARGYLES

L-101

LUTE RECORDS

ALLEY OOP
HULLY GULLY
HONKY TONK
YAKETY YAK
SHO' KNOW A LOT ABOUT LOVE
THE BUG EYED MAN

SO FINE
YOU'RE RUININ' MY GLADNESS
THE WAY I SEE IT
YOU'LL ALWAYS BE MY DARLING
GUN-TOTIN' CRITTER CALLED JACK
THE LOST RANGER

featuring
Gary Paxton

PRINTED IN U.S.A.

Michael Ochs Archives

ROCK ON

Paxton produced and released hundreds of records by young, new groups on his own label, Garpax, which released the hit "Monster Mash" (see #31). He also was a founder of Gardena Records. Paxton discovered Paul Revere and the Raiders at an A&W root beer stand in Boise, Idaho.

Paxton eventually moved to Nashville where he co-hosted a daily Christian talk show, recorded some gospel albums, and opened a Christian Youth Center and a recording studio. He's written or published cuts for country stars George Jones, Reba McEntire, and Mark Chesnutt.

Songwriter Dallas Frazier wrote and sang "Elvira," which reached #72 in 1966. Not until 15 years later, when the Oak Ridge Boys recorded it, did the song really score big. Their version reached #5 on the pop chart and #1 on the country chart.

Alley Oop

Oop oop oop oop oop
Alley oop oop oop
Oop oop

There's a man in the funny papers we
   all know
Alley oop oop oop
Oop oop.
He lives way back a long time ago
Alley oop oop oop
oop oop
He don't eat nothin' but a bear cat stew
Alley oop oop oop
Oop oop
Well this cat's name is Alley Oop

Alley oop oop oop
Oop oop.

He got a chauffeur that's a genuine
   dinosaur
Alley oop oop oop
Oop oop
And he can knuckle your head before
   you count to four
Alley oop oop oop
Oop oop
He got a big ugly club and a head full
   of hair
Alley oop oop oop
Oop oop
Likes great big lions and grizzly bears
Alley oop oop oop
Oop oop
He's the toughest man there is alive
Alley oop

Wearin' clothes from a wild cat's hide
Alley Oop
He's the king of the jungle jive
Look at that cave man go

He rides through the jungle tearin'
   limbs off of trees
Alley oop oop oop
Oop oop
Knockin' great big monsters dead on
   their knees
Alley oop oop oop
Oop oop
The cats don't bug him 'cause they
   know better
Alley oop oop oop
Oop oop
'Cause he's a mean motor scooter and
   a bad go getter
Alley oop oop oop
Oop oop

Alley Oop
He's the toughest man there is alive
Alley oop
Wears clothes from a wild cat's hide
Alley oop
He's the king of the jungle jive

There he goes.
Look at that caveman go. He sure is
   hip, ain't he? Like what's
   happening? He's too much. Ride
   daddy ride. Hi-yo dinosaur. Ride
   daddy ride. Get 'em man. Like
   hipsville.

TIE ME KANGAROO DOWN, SPORT

Rolf Harris

#15

FOR THE RECORD

Released by Epic Records in 1963.
Playing time: 3:02.
First became a top seller in England and Australia in 1961.
Reached #3 on the *Billboard* Hot 100 in 1963.

BACKGROUND MUSIC

This wacky Aussie tune was inspired by a calypso song sung by Harry Belafonte.

"It was written as a result of the Belafonte calypso craze that was sweeping the world in the 1950s," said Rolf Harris. "It impressed me enormously."

At the time, the Australian-born Harris played the piano and sang songs on children's television in England. He also performed one night a week at a night spot called The Down Under Club, which catered to Australians.

"I was trying to come up with new songs that had a simple chorus that everybody in the club could join in with," said Harris. Back then, Belafonte was riding a crest of popularity with his hit "Banana Boat (Day-O)" and had just recorded his follow-up "Hold 'Em Joe."

Recalled Harris, "I liked 'Hold 'Em Joe.' There was a line that went,

'Don't tie me donkey down there, let him bray, let him bray.' And I thought, 'That's good. I can change that and make it an Australian calypso. Instead of a donkey, I'll have a kangaroo in there somewhere.'

"Eventually, I came up with, 'Tie me kangaroo down, sport.' And the tune seem to come from midair. It was just handed to me on a plate."

Harris then sat down and wrote as many verses as he could think of that had anything to do with Australia. One of the verses was about a didgeridoo. "I heard of a didgeridoo but I didn't know what the hell it was," he admitted. He later learned that the didgeridoo is an oversized wooden pipe that drones when you blow on it.

Harris wrote 12 verses, but he cut some of them out like, "Let me gray dingo go, Dick/He can't stand the snow, Dick/ Boy, our kid's gone delirious/

That's not snow. That's his dandruff."

Harris sang the song publicly for the first time at The Down Under Club. "I didn't have the storyline, just a bunch of verses. And when I started singing it, I was booed. People shouted, 'Dreadful!' 'Stop singing it!' So I did. The next week at the club, someone shouted to me, 'Sing us that mad kangaroo song.' And I said, 'No one liked it.' He replied, 'I did. I thought it was good.' So I sang it again and this time everybody listened and seemed to like it. If it hadn't been for him, I probably never would've sung that song ever again."

Instead, Harris sang it every Thursday night at the club. Three years later, back in Australia, he sang the song on a TV show on a lark and received 200 letters from people asking for a copy of the lyrics.

"I then made a demo and played it for a friend in the record business. He listened to it and asked me, 'Where did you record this? In your bloody bathroom?' And I said, 'Yes I did, because it's the quietest room in the house.' He told me, 'These record peo-ple get 60 songs a week and if you don't impress them in the first few seconds, they throw it in the bin. Don't send them this crap. This is bloody dreadful. Get a studio and hire some musicians. At least do the best job you can.' So I did and I sent it off to Sydney and they put it out immediately. They used the demo as the record. Four weeks later, it was number one in Australia. It was amazing."

The song was a hit in England, too. But, said Harris, "It died a death in Canada in 1961—just disappeared without a trace." A year later, he wrote an aborigine-inspired song called "Sun Arise" which made it to #61 in the U.S. At the request of Epic Records, Harris sent them other songs, including "Tie Me Kangaroo Down, Sport." It was included on his new LP.

"A disc jockey in Denver played 'Tie Me Kangaroo Down, Sport' for a laugh," said Harris. "He told his audience, 'I don't understand the lyrics and I don't know what a didgeridoo is.' He got such a reaction to the song that he played it almost every hour. So Epic Records put it out as a single and it became a hit."

NOTEWORTHY NOTES

- Before it was recorded, the song was called "Kangalypso."
- The whoop-whoop-whoop sound in the background came from a wobbleboard—a thin sheet of Masonite that is held between the palms and shaken.
- Harris was so broke when he made the recording that he offered the backup singers 10 percent of the royalties. They demanded cash instead. So he paid them $15 apiece.
- Harris' brother Bruce came up with the idea of tying all the verses together into a story about a dying rancher. "There's a very macabre sense of humor in Australia," Harris said.

Michael Ochs Archives

■ Pat Boone was in Australia in 1961 when the song became a hit there. "When he returned to the United States, he told his record company he wanted to do the song," said Harris. "They said it was ludicrous and stupid and they talked him out of it. Then, when it became a hit in the U.S. in 1963, Pat came out with his own version. He was angry with his record company for not doing it earlier." Boone's version failed to make it onto the charts.

PLATTER PATTER

Rolf Harris used to perform with the Beatles—but it wasn't a pleasant experience for him.

In the early 1960s, he and the Fab Four shared the same producer, George Martin. (Martin produced the American version of "Tie Me Kangaroo Down, Sport" before dropping Harris to concentrate on the Beatles.) So Harris sometimes appeared as the emcee or opening act for the group.

"They didn't have much to do with me," said Harris. "But occasionally they mucked about with me. During one of my songs one night, they stood off in the wings with a microphone and made silly comments. I came storming off the stage and shouted, 'Get some bloody professionalism into you! You don't muck around with somebody else's act! Don't ever bloody do that again!' I was so angry. And after that, they didn't do it again, I can tell you!"

TIE ME KANGAROO DOWN, SPORT   129

ROCK ON

Rolf Harris, who splits his time between England and Australia, still writes and sings wacky songs. "I'm just a novelty-type guy doing weirdo bloody comedy," he said.

In 1993, he had a Top 10 hit in England with a version of Led Zeppelin's "Stairway to Heaven" musically molded after "Tie Me Kangaroo Down, Sport." His zany version features the sound of the wobbleboard and a chorus singing "All together now . . ." The record made it all the way to #7 in England.

Tie Me Kangaroo Down, Sport

There's an old Australian stockman
   lying dying
And he gets himself up onto one elbow
And he turns to his mates who are
   gathered around
And he says:

Watch me wallabies feed, mate
Watch me wallabies feed
They're a dangerous breed, mate
So watch me wallabies feed

All together now
Tie me kangaroo down, sport
Tie me kangaroo down
Tie me kangaroo down, sport
Tie me kangaroo down

Keep me cockatoo cool, Kool
Keep me cockatoo cool
Don't go away from the fool, Kool
Just keep me cockatoo cool

All together now
Tie me kangaroo down, sport
Tie me kangaroo down
Tie me kangaroo down, sport
Tie me kangaroo down

And take me koala back, Jack
Take me koala back
He lives somewhere out on the track,
   Mack
So take me koala back

All together now
Tie me kangaroo down, sport
Tie me kangaroo down
Tie me kangaroo down, sport
Tie me kangaroo down

Let me aboes go loose, Lou
Let me aboes go loose
They're of no further use, Lou
So let me aboes go loose

All together now
Tie me kangaroo down, sport
Tie me kangaroo down
Tie me kangaroo down, sport
Tie me kangaroo down

And mind me platypus duck, Bill
Mind me platypus duck
Oh, don't let him go running amuck,
   Bill
Just mind me platypus duck

All together now
Tie me kangaroo down, sport
Tie me kangaroo down
Tie me kangaroo down, sport
Tie me kangaroo down

Play your didgeridoo, Blue
Play your didgeridoo
Oh, like keep playing till I shoot
through, Blue
Play your didgeridoo

All together now
Tie me kangaroo down, sport
Tie me kangaroo down
Tie me kangaroo down, sport
Tie me kangaroo down

Tan me hide when I'm dead, Fred
Tan me hide when I'm dead
So we tanned his hide when he died,
Clyde
And that's it hanging on the shed

All together now
Tie me kangaroo down, sport
Tie me kangaroo down
Tie me kangaroo down, sport
Tie me kangaroo down

LOUIE LOUIE
The Kingsmen

#14

FOR THE RECORD

Released by Wand Records in 1963.
Playing time: 2:24.
Climbed to #2 on the *Billboard* Hot 100 where it stayed for six weeks.
Re-released in 1966; it reached #97.

BACKGROUND MUSIC

"Louie Louie" was a song with the foulest lyrics *never* written. Although the words were absolutely without offense, they *were* hard to understand, triggering a nationwide rumor that they were dirty. As a result, millions of listeners "heard" obscene lyrics that weren't ever sung on the record.

Los Angeles session singer Richard Berry wrote the tune in 1955. It was about a bartender named Louie who listens to a customer talk of his desire to go back home to his girlfriend in Jamaica. Berry recorded the song in 1956 as the "B" side to an R&B version of "You Are My Sunshine." That single didn't sell very well.

In 1961, entertainer Rockin' Robin Roberts found the record in the bargain bin of a store in Seattle. After he heard "Louie Louie," he cut his own version of the song. It became a popular number played by local rock bands throughout the northwest.

One of the groups that featured the song in its act was the Kingsmen,

whose gigs consisted of high school dances and supermarket openings in their hometown of Portland, Oregon. Guitarist Mike Mitchell and drummer Lynn Easton held day jobs at a food distributing firm whose owner let them use his Volkswagen van to cart around the band's equipment.

The Kingsmen played all the hit rock tunes of the day and ended their shows with "Louie Louie"—but as an instrumental. "It was a big five-minute closing number," Mitchell told the music magazine *Goldmine*. The song always drew raves from the audience. Once, at the urging of their fans during a 1963 appearance, the Kingsmen played "Louie Louie" for an entire 45-minute set! Although the band grew tired of playing the song for that long, the crowd loved it.

The next day, the Kingsmen went into a studio with local disc jockey Ken Chase and cut their own version of "Louie Louie" with the original lyrics. The group's vocalist, Jack Ely, had learned the words by listening to the song a few times on a jukebox.

"It was not set up as a music studio," recalled Easton. "It was just for voice-overs, mostly. They were not used to working with a rock group."

Mitchell said the studio didn't have the right equipment. "Everybody sat up and played at the same time with one microphone for each instrument and five on the drums. They hung a big mike from the ceiling and Jack had to stand on his toes to sing. Then they moved Jack back about four feet from the mike, and that's why you can't understand the words."

The Kingsmen cut the song in April, 1963, and got some local airplay. Eventually, the group made a deal with New York-based Wand Records, a label that featured black performers. "They had no idea we were white," said Mitchell. "By the time they found out we weren't black, the song was climbing up the *Billboard* chart. There's no picture of us on the first album because we were white."

NOTEWORTHY NOTES

- The day after the Kingsmen recorded "Louie Louie," Paul Revere and the Raiders—another Portland group—went into the same studio and cut their own version which became a regional hit.

- In 1985, the Washington state legislature voted down a resolution to make "Louie Louie" the state song.

PLATTER PATTER

The sensational rumor that the lyrics to "Louie Louie" were dirty started in the south.

"Some students at Tulane University called (drummer) Lynn's house one afternoon and said, 'We've heard the record and these are the words we hear. Is it true?' And then they sang some dirty lyrics," recalled Mitchell.

"That was the first time we learned that some people thought the lyrics were obscene because, in the northwest, it was a well-known song that had been played by many groups. The rumor spread to Florida, Indiana, and Michigan. It started with daughters telling their mothers, who went to their priests, who went to the governor who banned the record."

Allegedly, the dirty lyrics could only be heard at some other speed—33 or 78 or 16.

"That was really something," said Easton. "If we'd been able to do it, it would've been the greatest recording technique in the world—to have a record say something at one speed and something else at another.

"At one time we saw 35 different copies of the lyrics and they were all completely different, depending on what part of the country you were from."

Michael Ochs Archives

The rumor caused outrage in Indiana, where the governor banned the song from the state's airwaves. Eventually, the FCC and FBI launched an investigation and interviewed both Richard Berry and Jack Ely. The authorities concluded that the song was unintelligible at any speed.

FOLLOW UPS AND DOWNS

Among the Kingsmen's follow ups were "Money," #16, and "Little Latin Lupe Lu," #46, in 1964. Their second biggest hit was "The Jolly Green Giant," which peaked at #4 in 1965.

ROCK ON

The Kingsmen broke up in 1968 after being on the road about 300 days a year. Some of the members got back together for some gigs in 1983.

Louie Louie

Louie Louie
Oh no, me gotta go.
Louie Louie
Oh baby, me gotta go.

A fine little girl, she wait for me,
Me catch the ship across the sea.
I sailed the ship all alone,
I never think how I'll make it home.

Louie Louie
Oh no, no, no, me gotta go, oh no
Louie Louie
Oh baby, me gotta go.

Three nights and days I sailed the sea.
Me think of girl constantly.
On the ship I dream she there.
I smell the rose in her hair.

Louie Louie
Oh no, me gotta go, yeah, yeah, yeah,
* yeah.*
Louie Louie
Oh baby, me gotta go.

(Okay, let's give it to 'em right now!)

Me see Jamaica moon above.
It won't be long me see me love
Me take her in my arms and then
I tell her I'll never leave again.

Louie Louie
Oh no, me gotta go
Louie Louie
Oh baby, me gotta go.
I said we gotta go,
Let's get on outta here.
Let's go.

SHADDAP YOU FACE
Joe Dolce

#13

FOR THE RECORD

Released by MCA in 1981.
Playing time: 3:10.
Was an instant hit in Australia, but in the U.S., peaked at #53 on the *Billboard* Hot 100.
Sold over 3 million copies worldwide.

BACKGROUND MUSIC

Joe Dolce was inspired to write the classic send-up of life in an Italian-American family after a memorable visit to his Italian-born grandparents.

After two years of studying to be an architect at Ohio University, Dolce quit college and joined a rock and roll band called the Headstone Circus as lead guitarist. After drifting throughout the country and living in a couple of communes, Dolce moved to Australia.

In 1980, he returned to the United States to see his family. "I went to my grandparents' house for dinner and I was stunned by the way they talked," Dolce recalled. "I hadn't seen them in four years and I hadn't heard that sort of talk like 'Shaddap you face' and 'Whatsa matter you?'

"It just struck me that those phrases could turn into a good song. So on the way back to Australia, I began writing the song. I didn't think much more about it at the time."

Back in the land down under, Dolce starred in a progressive, experi-mental one-man cabaret act which was funded by a grant. One day, he decided to fine-tune "Shaddap You Face" and include it in his act. "It was more a fusion of acting and music because I created a character, Guiseppi—who talked with an Italian accent 'likea dis.' The audience loved it."

With the help of the grant, Dolce made a video and, prompted by the rave reaction of the cabaret audiences, tried to promote the song. "In those days, there were no music video channels," Dolce recalled. "My video was rejected everywhere, but finally I managed to get one morning TV show to play it and it created quite a stir. Soon, they were getting hundreds of calls from people wanting to see it again.

"It became a grass roots sort of phenomenon. All the TV shows that had rejected me started ringing me up, saying, 'Look, we've got to have you on.' 'The Don Lane Show'—which was the Australian equivalent of Johnny Carson's show—had rejected me. But once my song started getting the airplay, Don Lane announced on TV that he was going to have me on his show the next week—and that was before they even asked me!"

"Shaddap You Face" soared to the top of the charts in Australia and quickly became a hit throughout Europe. Eventually, the song began getting airplay in the United States, but it never attained the popularity it enjoyed in other countries.

"I gave up doing my cabaret act for about three years and just did television because the song was so big all over the world," recalled Dolce. "Every time the song began to slip on the charts in one country, it rose in another. I was flying from one country to another just to perform 'Shaddap You Face' on TV."

Dolce said that some of the Italians he met loved the song. But there were many people who took offense. "Basically, they reacted in very extreme ways," he said. "They threatened me. And a lot of places wouldn't let me perform it."

Among Italians who enjoyed the song were members of the Australian mafia. "I'll never forget the time I played in this mafia club," recalled Dolce. "There was this big table full of about 14 guys all looking like they'd come out of a grade B movie. I did the song and they loved it. They kept trying to get me to come with them after the show. I decided to pass."

NOTEWORTHY NOTES

- "Shaddap You Face" became a hit in 30 countries (including Italy) and was #1 in 15 of them.

- The song has been recorded in 20 different languages including Japanese, Chinese, and Greek. (The lyrics and accent were adapted to fit the nationality of each country.)

- The song has been performed by groups as diverse as a Hungarian gypsy band who sang it as a folk song to the English rock band EMF (they recorded the 1991 #1 hit "Unbelievable") who did a thrash version of it.

- "Shaddap You Face" was the biggest-selling record ever produced in Australia.

PLATTER PATTER

Joe Dolce once pinch-hit for the Pope!

It happened in 1981 shortly after Pope John Paul II was recovering from an assassination attempt.

"I went to Italy to sing 'Shaddap You Face' at an outdoor festival," Dolce recalled. "And the only reason I got invited there was because the Pope was supposed to attend, but he got shot a few days earlier.

"So at the last minute, they were looking for some performers to fill in. I agreed to do it. It was a bit of a scary feeling because I didn't know for sure how the people would react to my song. But they seemed to enjoy it at least as much as the opening act—a trained bear."

FOLLOW UPS AND DOWNS

Follow-up songs by Joe Dolce that, alas, went nowhere include: "Pizza Pizza," "You Toucha My Car And I Breaka You Face," "If You Wanna Be Happy" with Italian-American lyrics, and "I Saw Mommy Kissing Santa Claus" with Italian-American lyrics.

ROCK ON

Joe Dolce lives in Melbourne, Australia, his home since 1980. He has composed the music for several plays and scored two Australian feature films.

He and his long-time girlfriend, Linn Van Hek, often perform together on stage in socially relevant theatrical collaborations such as the much-acclaimed "Difficult Women." The duo give readings and sing songs celebrating famous women in history who dared to speak their minds.

A song he wrote with Van Hek

Joe Dolce

was used in the film *The Terminator*. "There's a scene in the movie where this girl is listening on her headphones to our song, 'Intimacy' and the Terminator comes in and shoots her," said Dolce. "The scene ends with the headphones lying on the floor with the music still playing and then the Terminator crushes it with his heel."

Shaddap You Face

Allo. I'm-a Guiseppe.
I got-a something-a special-a for you
Ready! Uno, due, tre, quatro

When I was a boy
Just about-a eighth-a grade
Mama used to say
"Don't-a stay out-a late
With the bad-a boys
Always shoot-a pool
Guiseppe gon' to flunk-a school"

Boy, you make-a me sick
All de ting I gotta do
I can't-a get-a no kicks
I always got to follow rules
Boy, it make-a me sick
Just to make-a lousy bucks
Got to feel-a like a fool

And-a Mama used to say all-a time:
"What's-a matter you? Hey!
Got-a no respect
Wadda-you tink you do
Why you look-a so sad
It's-a not so bad
It's-a nice-a place
Ah, shaddap-a you face."

That's-a my Mama, can-a remember
Big accordion solo
Play dat ting
Really nice, really nice

But soon-a come-a day
Gonna be-a big-a star
Den-a make-a T.V. shows and-a movies
Get-a myself a new car
But still I be myself
I don't-a want-a to change a ting
Still-a dance and-a sing

I tink about-a Mama, she used to say:
"What's-a matter you? Hey!
Got-a no respect

Wadda-you tink you do
Why you look-a so sad
It's-a not so bad
It's-a nice-a place
Ah, shaddap-a you face."

Mama, she said-a all-a de time:
"What's-a matter you? Hey!
Got-a no respect
Wadda-you tink you do
Why you look-a so sad
It's-a not so bad
It's-a nice-a place
Ah, shaddap-a you face."

'At's-a my Mama
Hello everybody 'ats out-a dere
In-a radio and-a T.V. land
Did you know I had a big-a
Hit-a song in-a Itality with-a dis
"Shaddap-a you face"
I sing-a dis-a song
All my fans applaud
Dey clap-a deir hands
Dat-a make-a me feel-a so good

You ought-a learn-a this-a song
It's-a real-a simple
See, I sing, "What's-a matter you?"
You sing, "Hey!"
Den I sing-a de rest
And den at de end
We can all-a sing
"Ah, shaddap-a you face."
O.K., let's-a try it really
Uno, due, tre, quatro

What's-a matter you? Hey!
Got-a no respect. Hey!
Wadda-you tink you do? Hey!
Why you look-a so sad? Hey!
It's-a not so bad. Hey!
It's-a nice-a place.
Ah, shaddap-a you face!

ITSY BITSY TEENIE WEENIE YELLOW POLKADOT BIKINI

Brian Hyland

FOR THE RECORD

Released by Leader Records in 1960.
Playing time: 2:19.
Soared to the top of the *Billboard* Hot 100 where it remained #1 for one week.

BACKGROUND MUSIC

Despite what innumerable listeners may have thought, "Itsy Bitsy Teenie Weenie Yellow Polkadot Bikini" was not about some buxom beach babe. It was about the two-year-old daughter of the writer of the song!

In 1959, songwriter Paul Vance took his daughter Paula to the beach. Watching her play in her yellow polkadot bikini, Vance became inspired to write a song about her beachwear. So he and collaborator Lee Pockriss came up with the music and lyrics.

Although Vance often sang on his own demos, he thought the song would sound better with a female vocal, so he hired a session singer and two other girls to back her up. The song was eventually obtained by record company owner Dave Kapp, who nevertheless worried that the tune was too risqué to release and expressed his concerns to Vance. The songwriter laughed and explained that the girl wearing the now legendary itsy bitsy teenie weenie yellow polkadot bikini was just two years old. Kapp agreed to release the song, but only after a change of artists.

Kapp thought that the song needed a male voice. He decided a New York teenager named Brian Hyland, whom his company had recently signed, should sing the lead.

Hyland, who grew up in a musically-inclined family of six boys and a girl, used to sing in the church choir. When he was in junior high school, he and some friends formed a group called the Del-Fi's. "We were interested in all the doo-wop sounds that were around at the time," Hyland recalled. "We would sing in subway stations and in store fronts around my neigborhood. We met a lot of girls that way.

"In 1958, we made a demo with money that we received at Christmas.

We'd cut a few classes and go to Manhattan and hit all the record companies we could in one day. We'd look in the Yellow Pages and go around knocking on doors. Usually, they'd say, 'Come back next week.'"

Eventually, Hyland met an arranger who convinced him to go solo. While working part time as an office boy for a publishing company called World Music, the teenager continued to cut demos, including one called "Rosemary."

"The demo was sent over to Kapp for a singer on his label to do," Hyland recalled. "But Kapp liked the way I did it. So I signed with him and made my first record at the age of 16."

A few weeks later, Kapp gave Hyland a copy of "Itsy Bitsy" on a demo sung by the three girls and asked him to record it for release. "They gave it to me on a Friday and I had to learn the song over the weekend," Hyland said. "We cut it on Monday.

"I was pretty relaxed during the recording session. Even though it wasn't really the kind of song that I usually liked, I had a feeling that it was special. When we recorded it, there seemed to be a real buzz in the air about the song."

Hyland will never forget the first time he heard the song on the radio. "I was driving with my brother Kenny and we were stopped at a traffic light at Howard Beach," he said. "A car pulled up beside us and the kids had the windows down and the radio blaring—and they were singing 'Itsy Bitsy.' I couldn't believe it. I like went into shock."

Suddenly, Hyland was hot. He began touring the country, performing live at state and county fairs, on local TV shows and Dick Clark's "American Bandstand." Meanwhile, the song, which reached the top of the charts in August, 1960, was the hit of the summer.

"Today when I hear the song, it sounds like somebody else singing it, because I was so young at the time," said Hyland.

NOTEWORTHY NOTES

- The recording session for "Itsy Bitsy" was so loose that one of the musicians was actually listening to a ball game while playing.

- Comedian Buddy Hackett also recorded the song at about the same time Hyland's was released, but Buddy's version never made it onto the charts.

- The song got a plug from the Three Stooges on their local New York TV show because Stooge Larry Fine was Brian's cousin.

- In the Billy Wilder film comedy *One, Two, Three*, starring James Cagney, the song was played over and over as a successful brainwashing technique

- When "Itsy Bitsy" became a hit, Brian appeared as a guest on the TV game show "To Tell The Truth."

PLATTER PATTER

Hyland was one of the last people to see President John F. Kennedy alive.

The singer was among the thousands of Americans who lined the streets in Dallas, waving to the President as he rode by on that fateful day, November 22, 1963.

"I was on tour in Dallas with Dick Clark, Bobby Vee, and the Ronettes," Hyland recalled. "I can remember the day very clearly. I was standing at the curb and watched Kennedy go by and I took a picture of him. Then I walked off and a couple of minutes later, I went into a store about a block away and I heard the terrible news on a little portable TV set that the President had been shot. That was one of the lowest moments of my whole life."

FOLLOW UPS AND DOWNS

Weeks after "Itsy Bitsy" hit #1, Brian Hyland recorded a follow-up that didn't come close to matching his earlier success. It was called "(The Clickity Clack Song) Four Little Heels." Hyland said he liked the flip side to the song better, "That's How Much."

However, Hyland did record 21 other songs which made the charts. He had two other Top 10 hits, "Sealed with a Kiss" in 1962 and a remake of The Impressions' "Gypsy Woman" in 1970. Both peaked at #3.

ROCK ON

Today Brian Hyland lives in the California high desert and continues to do live shows around the world.

"I really enjoy performing now more than I ever did when I was younger," he said. "It's a lot more laid back and a lot more fun. We have great equipment now that makes it a pleasure to go out and do a gig.

"I do all of my old hits. I do a real broad selection of classic rock and roll, too, like songs of Little Richard, the Everly Brothers, Jackie DeShannon, and Elvis."

Itsy Bitsy Teenie Weenie Yellow Polkadot Bikini

*She was afraid to come out of the
  locker
She was as nervous as she could be
She was afraid to come out of the
  locker
She was afraid that somebody would
  see.*

*Two, three, four
Tell the people what she wore.*

*It was an itsy bitsy teenie weenie
  yellow polkadot bikini
That she wore for the first time today
An itsy bitsy teenie weenie yellow
  polkadot bikini
So in the locker she wanted to stay.*

*Two, three, four
Stick around, we'll tell you more.*

*She was afraid to come out in the open
And so a blanket around her she wore
She was afraid to come out in the open
And so she sat bundled up on the shore.*

*Two, three four
Tell the people what she wore.*

*It was an itsy bitsy teenie weenie
  yellow polkadot bikini
That she wore for the first time today
An itsy bitsy teenie weenie yellow
  polkadot bikini
So in the blanket she wanted to stay.*

*Two three, four,
Stick around, we'll tell you more.*

*Now she's afraid to come out of the
  water
And I wonder what she's gonna do
Now she's afraid to come out of the
  water
And the poor little girl's turning blue.*

*Two, three, four,
Tell the people what she wore.*

*It was an itsy bitsy teenie weenie
  yellow polkadot bikini
That she wore for the first time today
An itsy bitsy teenie weenie yellow
  polkadot bikini
So in the water she wanted to stay.*

*From the locker to the blanket
From the blanket to the shore
From the shore to the water
Guess there isn't any more.*

BILLY, DON'T BE A HERO
Bo Donaldson & the Heywoods

#11

━━━━━━ FOR THE RECORD ━━━━━━

Released by ABC Records in 1974.
Playing time: 3:25.
Peaked at #1 on the *Billboard* Hot 100, where it remained for two weeks.
Sold 3 million copies.

━━━━━━ BACKGROUND MUSIC ━━━━━━

This syrupy, tear-jerking song about a soldier's heroic death during the Civil War turned into a modern-day, on-air battle of the bands.

"Billy, Don't Be a Hero" was first recorded by the British group Paper Lace in England, where it soared to #1 on the charts. But just days before Paper Lace cut a deal for American distribution, a Cincinnati band—Bo Donaldson & the Heywoods—came out with its own version of the tune in the United States.

DJs across the country played both cuts on the air and asked listeners to pick their favorite. Bo Donaldson & the Heywoods crushed Paper Lace.

Although the song was about the Civil War, it was written by two English composers, Mitch Murray and Peter Callander, who already had scored with such British invasion hits as "I'm Telling You Now," "How Do You Do It?" and "I Like It." After seeing a film about the War Between the States, they decided to write their heart-wrenching paean to battlefield sacrifice.

"We're both Yankophiles who were exposed to American music, films, and books in our formative years," Murray told reporters at the time. "Most of our songs are slanted toward the United States. Besides, the U.S. is where the money is. We approach our business the same way as if we were selling nuts and bolts."

While they were writing "Billy," Murray and Callander auditioned Paper Lace, which had just won a talent contest on a British television show. The group was signed up to the writers' own label, Bus Stop Records, and cut the single.

As the song climbed the English charts, Murray and Callander tried to make a deal to release the song in the U.S., but with little success. One record company told them, "You've sent us quite a few records. This is the worst one."

The writers offered the song to Jay Lasker, head of ABC Records, who was very interested, but the deal fell through. So Lasker decided to have one of his own groups sing a cover song—the music business term for recording someone else's record.

Recalled producer Steve Barri, "Lasker played me the song and said, 'Look, why don't we cover this thing? It's a great teen-oriented song.' When I expressed concern that it would be competing with Paper Lace's version, he said, 'We don't know when it's going to come out. It may be out tomorrow. It may be out in a month. We could beat them if we do one now.'"

ABC let Bo Donaldson & the Heywoods record "Billy." In the early seventies, the group had toured on Dick Clark's "Caravan of Stars" and had opened for such groups as the Rascals, Paul Revere and the Raiders, and Herman's Hermits. They had one charted single, "Special Someone," which reached #64 in 1972.

"Once the decision was made to have them record it, we went into the studio that very night and cut it," recalled Barri. "We had that record out within three days."

It was a good thing for Bo and the boys that ABC released the record as quickly as it did. Paper Lace's original version debuted in the U.S. only a week later. "The records were so similar," said Barri. "What was surprising to us was that since Paper Lace's record had been such a smash in Europe, you'd expect the radio stations here to play that version. But a lot of stations played both versions and let them battle it out on the air. The Heywoods always won.

"I don't know whether the Heywoods' record was better or not. I just think they had much bigger fan appeal here because they were getting tremendous exposure in the teen magazines."

While the Heywoods' song rocketed to the top of the charts, Paper Lace's version barely got airborne. It went only as high as #96.

"As I look back on it now," said Barri, "it's not the nicest thing in the world to have covered someone else's record like that. But it was something that was done quite a bit back then."

PLATTER PATTER

When Bo Donaldson & the Heywoods beat Paper Lace to the punch, it turned out to be a blessing in disguise for the English group.

After getting burned so badly by the Heywoods' version of "Billy," Paper Lace smartened up. Their next record, "The Night Chicago Died," was rushed out in the United States before any other group could release a cover version. As a result, the song—a Murray and Callander melodrama about

gangster Al Capone and his men shooting it out with the cops—rose all the way to #1.

"It might not have been number one if 'Billy, Don't Be a Hero' had been a hit by Paper Lace," claimed Murray. "People took notice of us because we were beaten to the post. It made more of a story for DJs to talk about."

As a promotional stunt, Paper Lace wrote to Chicago Mayor Richard Daley, hoping to get a warm welcome from him when they visited the Windy City on their tour. An aide for Daley responded with a nasty letter, suggesting that Paper Lace and the songwriters "jump in the Chicago River, placing your heads under water three times and surfacing twice. Pray tell us, are you nuts?"

Michael Ochs Archives

——— FOLLOW UPS ——— AND DOWNS

Bo Donaldson & the Heywoods followed up their hit with "Who Do You Think You Are" (#15) and "The Heartbreak Kid" (#39), both in 1974. The following year, they recorded "Our Last Song Together" (#95)—a prophetic title because they never made it onto the charts again.

——— ROCK ON ———

Songwriters Mitch Murray and Peter Callander remain in London where they continue to compose new tunes.

Bo Donaldson & the Heywoods disbanded in the late seventies and went their separate ways. Donaldson lives in California where he writes songs and occasionally performs in local gigs.

Billy, Don't Be a Hero

The marching band came down along
    Main Street
The soldier blues fell in behind
I looked across and there I saw Billy
Waiting to go and join the line.

And with her head upon his shoulder
His young and lovely fiancé
From where I stood I saw she was
    crying
And through her tears I heard her say,

"Billy, don't be a hero
Don't be a fool with your life
Billy, don't be a hero
Come back and make me your wife."
And as he started to go
She said, "Billy, keep your head low
Billy, don't be a hero
Come back to me."

The soldier blues were trapped on a
    hillside
The battle ragin' all around
The sergeant cried, "We've got to
    hang on, boys
We've got to hold this piece of ground.

"I need a volunteer to ride up
And bring us back some extra men."
And Billy's hand was up in a moment
Forgetting all the words she said.

She said, "Billy, don't be a hero
Don't be a fool with your life
Billy, don't be a hero
Come back and make me your wife."
And as he started to go
She said, "Billy, keep your head low
Billy, don't be a hero
Come back to me."

I heard his fiancé got a letter
That told how Billy died that day
The letter said that he was a hero
She should be proud he died that way
I heard she threw the letter away.

SHORT PEOPLE
Randy Newman

FOR THE RECORD

Released by Warner Brothers in 1977.
Playing time: 2:54.
Was Newman's first single to hit the *Billboard* Hot 100 when it soared to #2 and stayed there for three weeks.
Was a certified gold record.

BACKGROUND MUSIC

Ironically, Randy Newman's biggest hit was also his biggest headache. Of all the satirical songs that the curly-haired curmudgeon wrote, none was more controversial than "Short People." It caused such an uproar that he even received a death threat!

Newman has held a slightly warped view of society ever since he attended UCLA as a music major. He cut most of his classes because he could never find a parking place; he eventually dropped out of school a semester short of graduating. But he loved to write music. His first album, "Randy Newman," was released by Warner Brothers in 1968. It bombed so badly that the record company gave it away as a promotional item.

But the album trumpeted Newman as a songwriter with a bizarre sense of humor that made people think. Among the songs on the record was "Davy the Fat Boy," about a friend who promises to take care of Davy but ends up displaying him in a carnival sideshow. The song leaves listeners either laughing or stunned—or both.

Newman followed up with other albums, all of which also flopped—until his 1972 LP "Sail Away," which earned him a reputation for grim, absurdist satire. The title cut was essentially a sales pitch set in 18th-century Africa about the joys of slavery. The song "Political Science" advocated dropping the big one on South America "to see what happens."

Then, in 1974, Newman came down with a horrendous case of writer's block. He did nothing but sit around his house for more than two years—reading, watching TV, and playing with his two kids. "I was afraid I'd never write again," he said.

His agent Elliot Abbott cured Newman by booking him into the L.A. Amphitheatre in 1977. "I knew I would scare the shit out of him," Abbott told *Rolling Stone*. "We deliberately put tickets on sale early so when he said, 'I can't write anymore,' I could say, 'But we can't refund 3,300 tickets.' Then I would remind him of all those people screaming for new songs, and he would say, 'But you knew I was lying when I agreed to do this.'"

Newman finally did produce, but only after renting an office ten miles from his home and driving there every morning on the freeway. "I almost felt like part of the community," Newman said. "I'd never been able to establish a rhythm for working before. It was hard, real hard."

One of the songs he wrote, a single that was included on his next album, "Little Criminals," was "Short People." Its premise was simple: Short people have no reason to live. Although it was meant as a humorous statement against prejudice, not everyone took it that way. Of all the subjects he's tackled—rednecks, sexual dysfunction, child murderers, racism—listeners apparently found making musical cracks about one's size the most offensive.

During a tour stop in Memphis, Newman received a death threat because of the song. Remembering that Dr. Martin Luther King Jr. had been killed in Memphis, Newman hesitantly went through with the show crouched so closely to the piano that the audience could hardly see him. He didn't make much of a target for an average-sized assassin, let alone a short one.

Newman then made headlines by announcing, on an English radio program, that short men were so insecure they were dangerous and therefore should be abolished. He was joking, of course, but short people were once again outraged.

Mystified by the reaction of those who were offended, Newman tried to explain that his remarks had been meant as a joke. "It was only a throwaway idea, but it wasn't done consciously as a statement about prejudice," he told a reporter at the time. "It didn't seem like a big thing to me. TV people ask me if the song is about prejudice and I say 'Yeah.' But it's not very important. I become a wimp trying to explain it. But why should I? It's just a joke. I like my kids, and they're short."

Then Newman, who isn't short, added fuel to the fire by saying that the cut-off height for short people was 5 feet, 6 inches. "Wait a minute, I'm getting timid," he said. "Let's say 3 feet, 7 inches. Some little karate guy is likely to kick the shit out of me. I don't expect it to be a big commercial success in Japan."

Admitting that most of his music has "a high irritation factor," Newman claimed that "Short People" was misunderstood. "It's so bizarre," he said ten years later. "I mean, everyone should know nobody has anything against people because of their height. And if they do, then there's something wrong with them.

"The people in my songs are generally exaggerations. What they say and think is colored by who they are. When a song works, the audience understands the character's point of view. And they don't mistake it for mine."

— PLATTER PATTER —

Newman sports a heavyweight Hollywood lineage. The family tree includes studio executives, film music conductors, and arrangers. One uncle, Alfred Newman, won nine Academy Awards for his film scores, including *Anastasia* and *Airport*. Uncle Lionel conducted the Fox studio orchestra for years and won an Oscar for scoring *Dr. Doolittle*. And Uncle Emil helped score several John Wayne flicks.

— ROCK ON —

Newman has written hits for many other artists, including Bette Midler, Judy Collins, Joe Cocker, Bonnie Raitt, Ringo Starr, Gene Pitney, Ray Charles, Art Garfunkel, and Dusty Springfield.

He wrote the smash "Mama Told Me (Not To Come)" for Three Dog Night. "I was never crazy about that tune," Newman confessed. "The song is just about a fool at a party, that's all. I didn't think it would be a hit."

Michael Ochs Archives

Among his movie soundtrack gigs were *Parenthood*, *Three Amigos*, *The Natural*, and the Oscar-nominated *Ragtime*. (Newman also co-wrote the screenplay for *Three Amigos* and had a bit part in it. He played a singing bush!) He also scored several national TV commercials for such clients as Dr. Pepper, Nike, Nutrasweet, and Apple computers.

Short People

Short people got no reason
Short people got no reason
Short people got no reason
To live

They got little hands
Little eyes
They walk around
Tellin' great big lies
They got little noses
And tiny little teeth
They wear platform shoes
On their nasty little feet

Well, I don't want no short people
Don't want no short people
Don't want no short people
'Round here

Short people are just the same
As you and I
(A fool such as I)
All men are brothers
Until the day they die
(It's a wonderful world)

Short people got nobody
Short people got nobody
Short people got nobody
To love

They got little baby legs
And they stand so low
You got to pick 'em up
Just to say hello
They got little cars
That go beep, beep, beep
They got little voices
Goin' peep, peep, peep
They got grubby little fingers
And dirty little minds
They're gonna get you every time

Well, I don't want no short people
Don't want no short people
Don't want no short people
'Round here

THE PURPLE PEOPLE EATER

Sheb Wooley

#9

FOR THE RECORD

Released by MGM Records in 1958.
Playing time: 2:11.
Took only three weeks to soar to #1 on the *Billboard* Hot 100 and stayed there for six weeks.
Sold over 3 million copies.

BACKGROUND MUSIC

"The Purple People Eater," one of the fifties' wackiest tunes, almost didn't get recorded. The reason? No one, not even Sheb Wooley, who wrote and recorded the song, thought it was very good.

Wooley, raised on an Oklahoma cattle ranch, first became intrigued with music when he was 11 years old; he talked his dad into trading a shotgun for an old guitar. In high school, Wooley formed his first band, the Plainview Melody Boys, which played at local dances.

After World War II, Wooley set out on his own for Nashville with a folder full of songs he had written. Eventually, stars like Jimmy Dean and Hank Snow began recording his tunes. In 1948, Wooley recorded one of his own songs, "Peepin' Through The Keyhole, Watchin' Jole Blon," which became a hit in Texas.

Not until ten years later did he enjoy his first national hit, "The Purple People Eater"—a song inspired by a grade schooler's joke.

"I was having dinner with a friend of mine, Don Robertson, who's a songwriter," Wooley recalled. "He told me his son had come home from school with all these weird jokes like, 'What has one eye, one horn, and flies and eats people? A one-eyed, one-horned, flying people eater.' That's the first time I ever heard of such a thing.

"So I asked Don, 'Why don't we write a song about that?' And he said, 'Well, you go ahead. That's more in your field.' Since I had written a few novelty songs before, I sat down and wrote it, mostly for the fun of it."

A few days later, Wooley met with the bigwigs at MGM Records to go over new songs he had written. "I was singing mostly ballads," Wooley recalled. "But there was no great excitement in the room. Then the president of the company asked, 'What else do you have?' I looked in my guitar case where the music for 'The Purple People Eater' was and I told him, 'It's nothing you want to hear. It's the bottom of the barrel.'"

But at the president's urging, Wooley sang the song—and the head honcho liked it. But apparently few others in the company did. "After we recorded it, the people in charge of sales didn't want to release it," said Wooley. "They said, 'We don't want to be identified with this. We're Metro Goldwyn Mayer!'

"But they finally went ahead and released it. The song just broke wide open. It was an instant hit. In fact, they couldn't press copies fast enough."

Wooley later learned how important his zany song was to MGM Records. "The company was on its ass financially," he said. "They were about to go broke. But that summer, 'The Purple People Eater' put them back in business."

NOTEWORTHY NOTES

- Wooley recorded both the voice of the Purple People Eater and the saxophone track at a reduced speed, and then played them at a high speed for the record.

- Other record companies tried to capitalize on the song's success by releasing tie-in or "answer" re-

cords, such as Joe South's "The Purple People Eater Meets the Witch Doctor," which hit #47 in 1958.

- The song's popularity triggered a merchandising rampage which included Purple People Eater T-shirts, hats, horns, and even ice cream.

PLATTER PATTER

Sheb Wooley couldn't go on tour to promote the song because at the time he was busy co-starring in the TV series "Rawhide"—the show that made Clint Eastwood a star.

Wooley was not only a singer-songwriter but an accomplished actor as well who had appeared in dozens of movies. He had made his Hollywood debut in 1950 playing a bad guy in the Errol Flynn film *Rocky Mountain*. The following year, Wooley portrayed a whiskey-drinking killer in the classic *High Noon*, starring Gary Cooper, and later played a rancher in *Giant*.

In 1958, Wooley signed a contract with CBS to play the role of East-

wood's cattle-driving scout Pete Nolan in a pilot for the western "Rawhide." Recalled Wooley, "While the pilot was laying in the can and we were wondering whether it would ever air, I wrote 'The Purple People Eater.' Then, just when the record broke, they called me and said, 'OK, we're going to make the series.' So that tied me up and kept me from doing a lot of roadwork and personal appearances to plug the record."

Wooley stayed on the TV series for four and a half years of its six-year run. "Clint and I got along just beautifully," he said. "We were buddies. We partied around together and went water skiing. We had a great time."

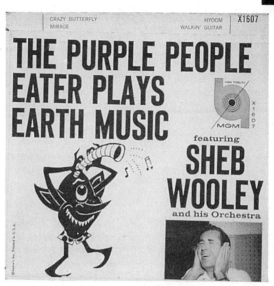

CRAZY BUTTERFLY
MIRAGE

HYOOM
WALKIN' GUITAR

X1607

THE PURPLE PEOPLE EATER PLAYS EARTH MUSIC

featuring **SHEB WOOLEY** and his Orchestra

FOLLOW UPS AND DOWNS

Sheb Wooley followed up "The Purple People Eater" with a few country and western songs such as "Sweet Chile" and "That's My Pa." But pop music fans wanted to hear his funny novelty songs instead. So he created an alter ego, a drunk named Ben Colder. Under the guise of Ben Colder, Wooley recorded parodies of hit songs including: "Hello Walls No. 2," "Harper Valley PTA (Later That Same Day)," and "Lucille No. 2." None of the parodies climbed higher than #58 on the charts.

ROCK ON

After the success of "The Purple People Eater" and his stint on "Rawhide," Wooley continued with music, recording many records and going out on tour, playing fairs and clubs. He toured U.S. bases during the Vietnam War. He continued his acting career as well, appearing in over 50 films. "The last major movie I appeared in was *Hoosiers*," he said. "It was probably my best work."

Now in his 70s, Wooley, who lives in a Nashville suburb, continues to work. In fact, he performs at a theater he co-owns near Opryland called the Jim Ed Brown Theater. "It's great fun," he said. "We have a great show."

The Purple People Eater

Well, I saw the thing a-comin' out of
   the sky
It had one long horn and one big eye
I commenced to shakin' and I said,
   "Ooh-wee,
It looks like a purple people eater to me."

It was a one-eyed, one-horned, flyin'
   purple people eater
One-eyed, one-horned, flyin' purple
   people eater
One-eyed, one-horned, flyin' purple
   people eater
Sure looked strange to me.

Well, he came down to earth and he lit
   in a tree
I said, "Mister purple people eater,
   don't eat me."
I heard him say in a voice so gruff,
"I wouldn't eat you 'cause you're so
   tough."

It was a one-eyed, one-horned, flyin'
   purple people eater
One-eyed, one-horned, flyin' purple
   people eater
One-eyed, one-horned, flyin' purple
   people eater
Sure looked strange to me.

I said "Mister purple people eater,
   what's your line?"
He said, "Eatin' purple people and it
   sure is fine
But that's not the reason that I came to
   land
I wanna get a job in a rock and roll
   band."

Well, bless my soul, rock 'n roll, flyin'
   purple people eater
Pigeon-toed, under-growed, flyin'
   purple people eater
He wears short shorts, friendly little
   people eater
What a sight to see.

And then he swung from the tree and
   he lit on the ground
And he started to rock, a-really rockin'
   around
It was a crazy little ditty with a
   swingin' tune
Singa bop bapa loop a lap a loom
   bam boom.

Well, bless my soul, rock 'n roll, flyin'
   purple people eater
Pigeon-toed, under-growed, flyin'
   purple people eater
He wears short shorts, friendly little
   people eater
What a sight to see.

Well, he went on his way and then
   what-a you know
I saw him last night on a T.V. show
He was blowin' it out, really knockin'
   'em dead
Playin' rock 'n roll music through the
   horn in his head.

Tequila!

156   Sheb Wooley

TELEPHONE MAN
Meri Wilson

#8

━━━━━ FOR THE RECORD ━━━━━

Released by GRT Records in 1977.
Playing time: 1:58.
Made it up to #18 on the *Billboard* Hot 100 and became a gold single.

━━━━━ BACKGROUND MUSIC ━━━━━

This breathless, giggly song filled with double entendres was actually about a real telephone man whom singer-songwriter Meri Wilson dated after he installed a phone in her apartment!

"I swore for years that I'd never admit in public that I dated the telephone man, but the truth is, yes, I did," revealed Meri. "So I wrote a silly song about it."

While growing up in the Atlanta area, Meri played classical music on the piano, cello, and flute. "I was real hung up on writing music that was music." But she did write some novelty songs just for the fun of it and kept them in a notebook.

After graduating from Indiana University, Meri moved to Dallas and into her first apartment. And that's where she met the telephone man. In recalling the moment, Meri said with a laugh, "I shouldn't say anything more about him because I'm happily married—but not to the telephone man." When pressed, she described how the song originated.

"As I was getting the telephone installed, I remembered a line in a song by Laura Nyro that goes like, 'I met him on a Sunday and kissed him on a Monday.'" So after Meri and the telephone man started dating, she wrote the song with all its clever double meanings.

Eventually, Meri began playing local clubs where she sang ballads in the style of Anne Murray and Crystal Gayle. But one day she showed the music and lyrics of "Telephone Man" to her backup musicians and they encouraged her to perform it live. "So I did," she said. "In nightclubs, people aren't real attentive, but I noticed that every time I did 'Telephone Man,' people would listen."

But Meri was still more interested in singing serious songs and soon cut some demos for producer Allen Reynolds. Recalled Boomer Castleman, one of the musicians for the session, "Meri sang four songs and as we were putting up our instruments, I heard her in the corner singing this goofy little song called 'Telephone Man.'"

Castleman urged her to sing it for Reynolds. "I did it a cappella with just fingersnaps and Allen was tickled to death," Meri recalled. "But he couldn't figure out what to do with it." So the idea of recording it was dropped.

Six months later, Castleman caught Meri's act at a Dallas nightclub where she sang "Telephone Man." He reintroduced himself to her. "I told Meri I really liked the song and I'd like to take her in the studio the next day and record it. And that's what we did."

Recalled Meri, "I didn't see the likelihood of this song becoming a hit and I didn't realize how unique the song was. Boomer went to 17 record companies and they all scoffed at the song and said, 'no way.' And Boomer told me, 'Don't worry. We'll create our own label and put it out.'"

Armed with hundreds of copies of the song in the back of his car, Castleman, who was now acting as Meri's manager, gave away the record to radio stations throughout Texas. He also handed out complimentary copies to the record stores that each station tracked. The plan worked.

"I was in a Dallas store when I heard 'Telephone Man,'" said Meri. "I was shocked. So Boomer and I kept calling the radio stations, acting as typical listeners and asking them to play the song again and again, thinking we would have an impact on the airplay."

The song became such a local hit that major record companies began calling Castleman about releasing it on their label. A deal was quickly cut with GRT Records for nationwide distribution, and the song became an instant hit.

Today, says Meri, she wishes her claim to fame had been a serious record rather than a novelty song. "It was fun to have a hit record, but in my heart I was really disappointed that I couldn't have had a real piece of music out there."

NOTEWORTHY NOTES

- The record was cut at a Dallas video studio at a total cost of $228.

- "The song you hear on the record is actually the first take that we did," said Meri. "The tempo got faster and faster on that first take so we kept redoing it, but we ended up liking the first one best."

- The song was so popular the first few weeks that some stations played it too often, annoying many listeners. "I heard that some disc jockeys were threatened with death if they played it again," said Meri.

PLATTER PATTER

Meri is a natural-born comedienne who promoted "Telephone Man" by doing interviews, pretending to be as ditzy as she sounded on the record.

"I had a lot of fun," she said. "All I had to do was act stupid."

But sometimes she blundered big time on radio interviews—and it wasn't an act.

"I always got the station's call letters screwed up," she said. "One day, we were in Nashville and I did interviews on two different stations, WMAK and their rival WLAC. The people at WLAC asked me to do a promo for them live, so I said, 'Thanks for listening to WMAK.' And right then, the power went off at the radio station!"

To this day, Meri doesn't know if it was a coincidence or if it happened on purpose. "Boomer thought they got mad and shut down the radio station because of what I said. It was a very awkward moment."

PHOTO COURTESY: BCI/Amrita Music

FOLLOW UPS AND DOWNS

Meri Wilson followed up her hit novelty record with a traditional song called "Midnight in Memphis" that failed to make the charts. "I loved that song, but it didn't do that well," she said.

Then Meri came back with "Peter The Meter Reader." Said Meri, "We asked ourselves, 'How do we follow 'Telephone Man'?' And we thought, 'With another utility man. Like a meter reader.'" At the end of the song, the meter reader turns out to be the former telephone man. The song failed to make it onto the charts.

ROCK ON

Today Meri Wilson is the choral director of a high school in Atlanta.

"I also sing in a professional jazz group called the Hotlanta Jazz Singers," she said. "One of the guys in the group used to sing with the Four Freshmen." In addition, Meri sings on locally-produced commercials.

Telephone Man

*I rented my apartment on a Monday at
one.*
*Singing do la li la li shiki bum shiki
bum.*
*Starting moving in it on a Tuesday at
two.*
Singing do la li la li shiki do shiki do.

*Wednesday at three I called the phone
company,*
*Singing, hey baby, put a phone in for
me.*
Thursday at four
*He came a-knocking on my door
singing*

Hey baby,
I'm your telephone man,
You just show me where you want it
And I'll put it where I can
I can put it in the bedroom,
I can put it in the hall,
I can put it in the bathroom,
I can hang it on the wall
You can have it with a buzz
You can have it with a ring
And if you really want it
You can have a ding-a-ling.
*Because hey, baby, I'm your telephone
man.*

*Can you believe that? And then he
says,*
"Now when other fellas call
You tell 'em how it all began."

My heart began a-thumping
And my mind began to fly
*And I knew I wasn't dealing with no
ordinary guy.*
*So while he was a-talking I was
thinking up my plan*
Then my fingers did the walking
On the telephone man,
Singing hey la li la li, hey la li la li,
Hey la li la li, get it any way you can.
Right? So . . .

I got it in the bedroom
And I got it in the hall
And I got it in the bathroom
And he hung it on the wall.
*I got it with a buzz and I got it with a
ring*
*And when he told me what my number
was*
I got a ding-a-ling.
*Singing hey la li la li, hey la li la li,
hey la li la li.*
Just a-doing my thing.

I never did anything like this before.

(YOU'RE) HAVING MY BABY

Paul Anka with Odia Coates

#7

━━━━━━━━ FOR THE RECORD ━━━━━━━━

Released by United Artists in 1974.
Playing time: 2:32.
Remained #1 on the *Billboard* Hot 100 for three weeks.
Sold over 3 million copies.

━━━━━━━━ BACKGROUND MUSIC ━━━━━━━━

It seemed innocent enough. All Paul Anka wanted to do was write a tender tune celebrating pregnancy. Instead, he conceived a song that outraged pro-lifers, pro-choice advocates and feminists alike—and climbed to the top of the charts at the same time.

Anka's early songs were flak-proof. As a teenage heartthrob, he wrote and recorded safe adolescent songs, including two huge #1 hits, "Diana" in 1957 and "Lonely Boy" in 1959. Just about every one of his early-sixties teen love songs became a hit.

But then Anka's recording career went into a decade-long funk. In 1974, he was looking for a song that would ignite his comeback when he thought of his wife and their four daughters. "I had to come back with a big hit, and all I had to fall back on was my own experience," he once told *Time*. "What I experienced was four natural childbirths." So he sat down and wrote what he considered a sentimental song about the joys of impending fatherhood.

To his amazement, Anka discovered his song was about to give birth to a major controversy over its unapologetically proprietary tone. The problem first arose after the tune was played for a pre-release focus group. Full-fledged protests followed.

"I was well aware from the start that the song was going to offend certain people," Anka told reporters. "But, hell, you can't please everybody. I wrote that song for myself and about myself. But you know, men really do say 'my' baby. It's only natural."

Feminists labeled Anka a male chauvinist and his lyrics disgustingly sexist. He didn't help matters when he told the press, "I got the kind of flak I expected. We tested it on some chicks first and got all kinds of objections."

Offended by the title, the lyrics, and remarks like that, the National Organization for Women awarded Anka one of its annual "Keep Her in Her Place" awards. Ellen Peck, the founder of the National Organization for Non-

Parents declared, "Were I 16 and pregnant, that song could keep me pregnant."

The former teen idol infuriated both the right-to-lifers and the pro-choice set, who objected to different parts of the same lyrics: "You didn't have to keep it / Wouldn't have put you through it / You could have swept it from your life / But you wouldn't do it."

Anka had to defend himself at most every interview he held during his promotional tour. "I wasn't putting women in a subservient position, for God's sake," he declared at the time. "Motherhood is a fact of life. It's the personal statement of a man caught up in the affection and joy of childbirth.

"There is a time when a man feels that a woman is having his baby," Anka went on. "I know because I am married and have four kids. When I did the song, I knew what I was letting myself in for. But it's selling records and some of the people who bought it have to be women.

"It's strange that people can sing about war, drugs, and sex and get no flak. But sing about motherhood and right away some people are screaming and yelling. I'm seriously thinking of waiting about six months and putting out a song with the same melody as 'Having My Baby' and calling it 'You're Killing My Baby.' I'd write it abortion style. You can imagine the flak I'll get about that one if the stations have enough guts to play it."

But the criticism of his song did affect him. During a concert tour following the release of the song, Anka made one concession to his critics. He changed the lyric to the more inclusive ". . . having *our* baby."

NOTEWORTHY NOTES

Paul Anka set the mark for the longest time between number one singles by the same recording artist—15 years, 2 weeks. That's how long it had been from the time "Lonely Boy" was at the top of the charts to the day "(You're) Having My Baby" became #1. (The record has since been broken by the Beach Boys who went 24 years and four months between #1 hits—"I Get Around" in 1964 and "Kokomo" in 1988.)

PLATTER PATTER

Paul Anka originally planned to record "(You're) Having My Baby" as a solo. But he wound up doing it as a duet with Odia Coates, who had previously worked with Sly and the Family Stone.

"Much of the song's success is due to Odia," Anka claimed. "When I was recording it as a solo, we felt it needed a personal touch, and she was it."

Anka first met Coates when he was composing the song. At the time, she was a young married mother of two children doing gigs in various clubs and as a session singer. A mutual friend had arranged for Coates to audi-

Michael Ochs Archives

tion for Anka, who was producing records as well as writing songs. She knocked him out with her renditions of "Do You Wanna Dance" and "If You Really Love Me." As a result, he eventually hired her for a featured spot in his nightclub act in Las Vegas.

A few months later, when Anka was set to record "(You're) Having My Baby," he invited Coates to the studio in New York. "I went there just to sit in," she recalled. "Paul and a record executive were talking and they decided that the song needed a feminine touch. Well, since I was sitting there, they asked me to try out some lyrics. So I sang, 'I'm a woman in love, and I love what it's doing to me.' And they thought it would work—and it did. That was a big break for me."

FOLLOW UPS AND DOWNS

Anka and Coates followed up their hit with "One Man Woman/One Woman Man," which reached #7 in 1975. Later that same year, they recorded "(I Believe) There's Nothing Stronger Than Our Love" which made it to #15.

As for Anka's solo work, "I Don't Like To Sleep Alone" climbed to #8 in 1975. "Times of Your Life" rose to #7 in 1976 (and later became the theme song of a popular Kodak commercial).

Coates' only charted solo was the Anka-produced "Showdown," which made it to #71 in 1975.

─────── ROCK ON ───────

Paul Anka continues to do what he's done for decades—write music for himself and others, perform in night-clubs, and produce records. Tragically, Odia Coates' life was cut short when she died of cancer in 1991.

(You're) Having My Baby

Having my baby
What a lovely way
Of saying how much you love me
Having my baby
What a lovely way
Of saying what you're thinking of me

I can see it
Your face is glowing
I can see it in your eyes
I'm happy knowing
That you're having my baby

You're the woman I love
And I love what it's doing to you
Having my baby
You're a woman in love
And I love what's going through you

The needs inside you
I see it showing
Oh, the seed's inside you baby
Do you feel it growing
Are you happy knowing
That you're having my baby

I'm a woman in love
And I love what it's doing to me
Having my baby
I'm a woman in love
And I love what's going through me

Didn't have to keep it
Wouldn't put you through it
You could have swept it from your life
But you wouldn't do it
No, you wouldn't do it
Now you're having my baby

I'm a woman in love
And I love what it's doing to me
Having my baby
I'm a woman in love
And I love what's going through me

Having my baby
What a lovely way
Of saying how much you love me
Having my baby
I'm a woman in love
And I love what's going through me

PAC-MAN FEVER
Buckner & Garcia

#6

FOR THE RECORD

Released by Columbia Records in 1982.
Playing time: 3:43.
Peaked at #9 in the *Billboard* Hot 100.
Became a gold single.

BACKGROUND MUSIC

Two writers of radio jingles were taking a break and playing the latest rage in video games—Pac-Man—when a producer friend said, "Hey, why don't you turn this into a song?"

"We didn't want to at first," said Jerry Buckner. "But we finally wrote it and it became a big Top 20 hit for us."

Buckner and his partner Gary Garcia first met in high school in Akron, Ohio, where they each had their own band. "Gary played guitar for the Outlaws and I played keyboard for my band, the Rogues," recalled Buckner.

"We both had the same dreams and desires. Akron used to be a big industrial town with rubber factories and after graduation most guys worked for those folks. We wanted to get out of that life and we thought music was the way to do it. We used to drive around town all the time and dream of writing hit songs."

In the mid seventies, Buckner and Garcia moved to Atlanta where they wrote jingles for radio commercials and penned songs on the side. "If we liked an idea, we'd just do it," Buckner said. "We didn't think in terms of 'Does this make commercial sense? Is it smart to waste your time on this? Are we going to make money on this?'"

One of the ideas they liked was "Merry Christmas in the NFL," a novelty tune imagining sportscaster Howard Cosell as Santa Claus. The duo got a local DJ to record the song and it sneaked onto the charts, topping off at #82. "One day we heard they were going to play the song at halftime on 'Monday Night Football,'" Buckner said. "We sat in front of the TV, chewing our nails, waiting to hear the song, but they never played it. Later, we learned Cosell was offended by the record and wouldn't let them play it on the air."

In 1980, the writing team composed "Footprints in the Sand," a sentimental song that made its way onto the country charts. As a result, Buckner and Garcia were hoping to pen more tunes for the pop charts.

One day, while they were playing

the video game "Pac-Man," a friend of theirs, record producer Arnie Geller, told them they had a potential song idea right in their hands. "He reminded us that this Pac-Man thing was big," said Buckner. "But we didn't really want to do any more novelty tunes because we had tons of other good songs we wanted to record.

"A few days later, I was sitting at the piano, messing around, and I wrote some verses and a chorus for 'Pac-Man Fever.' The next day, I played the song to Gary and he said, 'I love the chorus, but the verses suck.' So we messed with the verses and then played them for Arnie. He went crazy and said, 'That's a great song. Let's record it.'

"We cut the thing, but only after we kept changing the lyrics at the last minute. Then we sent the track to all the major record companies, and every single one of them turned us down. I've still got the letters like, 'Thanks for considering us, but we don't think this has any commercial value' or 'It doesn't sound like a hit.'

"So Arnie put the record out himself on BGO Records and a local station played it and the request lines lit up. By the end of the week, we had sold thousands of singles. It was unbelievable. About a week later, Columbia Records said they wanted the record and made a deal with us. That's when the song became a national hit."

Buckner and Garcia plugged the song on national TV shows including their all-time favorite, "American Bandstand."

"It was so much fun to do—and so scary," said Buckner. "I remember Gary saying, 'You watch this show all your life and all of a sudden you're on it.' Before the show, which had moved to Los Angeles, Dick Clark came in and I was in such awe of him that I started tensing up. He did a little pre-interview with us first and when he asked us some questions, we just stared at him. He told us, 'Guys, you're going to have to talk if this is going to work.'

"After he left, I turned to our manager and said, 'I can't do this. It's not fun anymore. I'm scared to death.' But we went out there and did it. I must have really blanked out, because I don't remember what I said. But it was a wonderful experience.

"Afterwards, they had paid for a car and driver for us and we were driving down Rodeo Drive and Gary and I looked at each other and started laughing. I said, 'Not bad for a couple of yokels from Akron.'"

PLATTER PATTER

On the song, the sound of Pac-Man gobbling up dots was recorded off a video machine. "We sent a guy out to get the actual sound that Pac-Man makes on the video, so he went to the nearest deli shop and recorded it there," said Buckner.

"If you listen real close, you can hear a patron actually ordering a sandwich very faintly in the background. That wasn't intentional."

Michael Ochs Archives

FOLLOW UPS AND DOWNS

When Columbia Records released "Pac-Man Fever" (Buckner and Garcia's only charted single), the label wanted it followed up quickly with an album. The duo had only four weeks to compose, write, and record an LP featuring songs about video games.

"We went out and played the games so we could get a feel for them," said Buckner. "We learned all the terms and characters and came up with ideas for the songs."

The album, called "Pac-Man Fever," included such tunes as "Ode to a Centipede," "Goin' Berserk," "Do the Donkey Kong," and "Froggy's Lament." It was a modest success, peaking at #24.

ROCK ON

In 1986, Jerry Buckner wrote Anne Murray's country hit "On and On." Although he still composes songs on the side, he spends most of his time writing and producing comedy material for radio.

Pac-Man Fever

I got a pocket full of quarters
And I'm headed to the arcade
I don't have a lot of money
But I'm bringing everything I made

I got a callus on my finger
And my shoulder's hurting too
I'm gonna eat 'em all up
Just as soon as they turn blue

'Cause I got Pac-Man fever
It's driving me crazy
I got Pac-Man fever
I'm going out of my mind
I got Pac-Man fever
I'm going out of my mind

I've got all the patterns down
Up until the ninth key
I got Speedy on my tail
And I know it's either him or me

So I'm heading out the back door
And in the other side
Gonna eat the cherries up
And take them all for a ride

I got Pac-Man fever
It's driving me crazy
I got Pac-Man fever
I'm going out of my mind
I got Pac-Man fever
I'm going out of my mind

I'm gonna bank to the left
And move to the right
'Cause Punky's too slow
And Bunky's out of sight

Now I've got 'em on the run
And I'm looking for the high score
So it's once around the block
And I slide back out the side door

I'm really cooking now
Eating everything in sight
All my money's gone
So I'll be back tomorrow night

'Cause I got Pac-Man fever
It's driving me crazy
I got Pac-Man fever
I'm going out of my mind
I got Pac-Man fever
Driving me, driving me
Driving me, driving me crazy

Pac-Man fever
I'm going out of my mind
Pac-Man fever
It's driving me crazy
I got Pac-Man fever
I'm going out of my mind

YOU KNOW MY NAME (LOOK UP THE NUMBER)

The Beatles

#5

FOR THE RECORD

Released by Apple as the "B"-side to "Let It Be" in 1970.
Playing time: 4:19.
"Let It Be" reached #1 on the *Billboard* Hot 100 and sold over 1.5 million copies.

BACKGROUND MUSIC

The Beatles' most bizarre song was nothing more than a musical joke inspired by a London telephone book. Although the lyrics are basically nothing more than a repetition of the song's title, the record took three years to complete.

"That was a piece of unfinished music that I turned into a comedy record with Paul [McCartney]," John Lennon said in a *Playboy* interview. "It was going to be a Four Tops kind of song—the chord changes are like that—but it never developed and we made a joke of it."

It all began back in the fall of 1966 when McCartney was working on the music of an untitled Motown-like song. He hadn't done much with it—until one day when Lennon, visiting McCartney's house, ambled over to the piano where a London phone book was resting. His eyes caught a slogan on the cover which read, "You

know the name, look up the number." He told McCartney he had an idea.

"John said to me, 'I've got a new song,'" McCartney told Beatles historian Mark Lewisohn years later. "'What are the words?' I asked.

"'You know my name, look up the number.'

"'No, what's the rest of it?'

"'No, no other words. Those *are* the words. And I want to do it like a mantra!'"

So Lennon began toying with a simple set of chord changes on the piano while repeating the title again and again. But after taping a demo at his home, he set it aside to work on "Strawberry Fields Forever."

Several months later, in May of 1967, the Beatles went back into the studio at Abbey Road to lay down the strange backing track of "You Know My Name." Having written no more words for the song, Lennon decided to make the track an offbeat work of art. He was motivated by the zany background sounds and goofy voices that often accompanied the music of an English group known as the Bonzo Dog Doo Dah Band whom the Beatles had worked with in their 1967 TV special "Magical Mystery Tour."

"You Know My Name (Look Up the Number)" had a long and involved recording history. The master tape was a composite of five different parts, each recorded separately. The first part—featuring guitars, drums, bass, hand claps, bongos, and a little vocal work—took fourteen takes. The tenth take was marked the best.

A few weeks later, the Beatles returned to the studio to work on the song again. They did more than two dozen takes of what turned into a fun-filled jam session with a flute, electric guitar, drums, organ, and tambourine. The song, still lacking a vocal track, was left on the shelf, unfinished, for two years.

Then in April, 1969, Lennon and McCartney finally got around to over-dubbing the vocals and sound effects. "McCartney looked back on this as his favorite Beatles session," wrote Beatles historian John Robertson. "It certainly sounds like they were having

fun, with Lennon twisting his voice into an array of Peter Sellers-like characterizations in response to McCartney's nightclub crooning."

The end result was a patchwork of seemingly disconnected bits of irreverent jamming. The opening section of "You Know My Name" features a heavy staccato piano and echoed drums. The song moves abruptly into a bossa nova rhythm and then takes on the sound of what one critic called "an outtake from a bird warblers' convention." From there, the music returns to a Latin shuffle and finishes off with a saxophone solo and some spirited belching.

Although the relationship between John and Paul had been getting increasingly strained at the time, this silly song seemed to bring them closer. They worked well together and even sang at the same microphone at the same time—something they hadn't done in recent sessions.

Recalled McCartney, "We just had these endless, crazy, fun sessions. And eventually we pulled it all together and we just did a skit. It was just so hilarious to put together. It's not a great melody or anything. It's just unique. It's probably my favorite Beatles track. Just because it's so insane."

NOTEWORTHY NOTES

- Brian Jones of the Rolling Stones played saxophone on the record.

- Ringo Starr was not around for one of the sessions, so Beatles roadie Mal Evans helped out in the

rhythm section—by shaking gravel in a tray.

- "Let It Be"/"You Know My Name (Look Up the Number)" was the next-to-last single ever released by the Beatles. The day before it reached #1, the Fab Four announced they were breaking up. In June of 1970, the Beatles' final release as a group, "The Long and Winding Road," reached #1 on the charts.

—— PLATTER PATTER ——

Some time before the song's debut as the "B" side to "Let It Be," John Lennon tried to release "You Know My Name"—not as a Beatles tune but as a single by the Plastic Ono Band, featuring Lennon and his wife Yoko Ono.

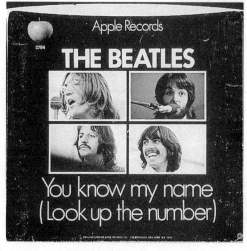

After the song had been basically finished in April of 1969, it was shelved for several months, much to Lennon's dismay. He decided that if the Beatles wouldn't release it, then he would. After all, it was his song.

On November 26, John and Yoko went into the studio. From 7 p.m. to 3 a.m., they edited and re-mixed "You Know My Name." He then made a test pressing of the song with another long-ignored tune of his, "What's The New Mary Jane," on the flip side.

Apple Records announced a rush release date of December 5 and in-formed the press that the record featured John and Yoko singing with support from a group of "many of the greatest show business names of today."

But the record was never released. Since the song had been recorded by the Beatles, George, Paul and Ringo weren't eager to give the Plastic Ono Band the credit. EMI, Apple's distributor, agreed with them.

Three months later, "You Know My Name" ended up on the flip side of "Let It Be."

You Know My Name (Look Up the Number)

You know my name,
Look up the number.
You know my name,
Look up the number.
You, you know,
You know my name.
You, you know,
You know my name.

Good evening and welcome to
* Slaggers*
Featuring Dennis O'Bell.
Come on, Ringo.
Here we go.
Let's hear it for Dennis. Hey!
Good evening.

You know my name,
Better look up my number.
You know my name,
That's right, look up my number.
You, you know,
You know my name.
You, you know,
You know my name.
You know my name,
Ba ba ba ba ba ba ba ba ba ba,
Look up the number.
You know my name,
That's right, look up the number.

Oh you know,
You know you know my name.
Huh huh huh huh.
You know my name,
Ba ba ba pum,
Look up the number.

You know my name,
Look up the number.

You, you know,
You know my name.
Baby, you, you know,
You know my name.
You know, you know my name.
You know, you know my name.

Go on, Dennis.
Let's hear it for Dennis O'Bell.

You know, you know,
You know my name.
You know, you know,
You know my name.
Prrr, you know my name,
Look up the number.
You know my name,
Look up the number.
You know, you know my name,
Look up the number.

You know my number three,
You know my number two,
You know my number three,
You know my number four,
You know my name,
You know my number, too.
You know my name,
You know my number
What's up with you?
You know my name.
That's right.
Yeah.

DISCO DUCK

Rick Dees and His Cast of Idiots

FOR THE RECORD

Released by RSO Records in 1976.
Playing time: 3:15.
Reached #1 on the *Billboard* Hot 100 for one week.
Remained on the charts for 25 weeks.
Sold over 2 million.

BACKGROUND MUSIC

When Rick Dees went into the studio to record "Disco Duck," the session musicians thought he was nuts.

"They were laughing *at* me, not with me," admitted Dees. "Actually, they thought I was an idiot."

At the time, Dees was the top-rated disc jockey for Memphis station WMPS—and one of the zaniest jocks anywhere. To promote his show, he dreamed up wacky world records, including the world's largest fruitcake (3,000 pounds), the world's largest jelly donut (300 pounds), the world's largest lollipop (150 pounds), and the world's largest T-shirt (9 feet by 14 feet).

While he was on this riotous roll, Dees thought the time was ripe to cash in on the current disco craze with a parody song. "Ken Pruitt, one of the guys who worked out at the same gym I did, could do a great duck voice," Dees recalled. "Then I remembered that there was a song back in the sixties called 'Do the Duck.' So I thought, 'Gee, how about 'Disco Duck'?"

"So I went back to my apartment and sat down and put my feet up on the chair because I had a problem with mice—and nobody likes to have their feet dangling when there might be a mouse running around—and wrote the song. It took me one afternoon to do."

He took the song to Estelle Axton, head of Fretone Records, a local label that had released an earlier Dees effort called "The National Wet Off." Recalled Dees, "That song was a bomb and it took me three months to convince them to try with 'Disco Duck.'" Axton finally agreed to set Dees up with three top session musicians to record some of his funny tunes, including "Disco Duck."

"I went into the studio with a bunch of song ideas—all of them warped," he recalled. "First, I hit them with my song about Elvis exploding called, 'He Ate Too Many Jelly Donuts.' The musicians just said, 'Man, have you got anything else?'

"I said, 'Here's the biggie: 'Disco

Duck.' I told them I had this vision of a dance-crazy duck with platform-webbed feet and a shag-feather cut. They just laughed, but I could tell they weren't laughing with me. But they humored me and laid down this good Memphis groove." His friend, Ken Pruitt, did the voice of the duck.

The record broke out of Birmingham and spread throughout the south. Ironically, it was getting airplay everywhere except in Dees' own Memphis. "Nobody would play it there because I was on the radio and the competition didn't want to promote me," said Dees. "And my own station thought it would be a conflict of interest if I played my own song."

The record proved to be too much for Fretone's limited facilities, so Dees went shopping for a new label. But everyone passed on the song. A friend, Roy Mack, then leaned on Al Coury, president of RSO Records.

Recalled Coury in a 1976 *Rolling Stone* interview, "I told Roy I didn't even want to hear it because it was by someone in radio, and if I didn't like it, I might make an enemy. But Roy wouldn't take no for an answer and I owed him favors."

Coury liked the record in spite of himself, but he didn't want to break his policy against making a deal with a DJ. Then Coury played it for his children—and they loved it. "I don't generally use my kids as a barometer, but I've got to admit, they made me think about the universal appeal this thing had," he said. Coury paid Fretone $3,500 for the record and soon discovered he had a big hit.

Dees claimed he wasn't surprised by the success of the song. "That's only because I was so naive. I didn't know anything about the record business back then. So I just assumed that you put out a song and it becomes a hit. When RSO released it, I felt it was going to be a smash."

PLATTER PATTER

"Disco Duck" did more than vault Rick Dees into the national spotlight. It also got him fired!

Memphis radio station WMPS, which soared to the top of the ratings because of Rick Dees' growing popularity, showed its gratitude by canning him from his DJ job.

"It's the song that fired me," he said. "To put it simply, the Duck did it.

"It bothered me that the record was playing everywhere but in Memphis. I didn't like the fact that my own station refused to let me play the record or promote it on the air. I suppose they felt that I would get a big head and become difficult to deal with. They were right," he joked.

Then one day, he told his listeners that he was going on a trip to Hollywood to promote "Disco Duck." Recalled Dees, "The station manager came in and even though I was doing real well in the ratings, he said, 'We think it's a conflict of interest and you're fired.'

"I wasn't out of work long—because I went to work for their competition."

— FOLLOW UPS AND DOWNS —

After the stunning success of "Disco Duck," Rick Dees failed to come up with any other hits.

He released "Dis-Gorilla"—a disco spoof coinciding with the latest film version of *King Kong*—which made it to #56 in 1977. Another record, "Barely White"—a takeoff on singer Barry White—did well in the Los Angeles area but failed to chart nationally. In 1984, Dees' record "Eat My Shorts/Get Nekked" stalled at #75.

——— ROCK ON ———

Ever since his stint in Memphis, Rick Dees has been one of the most popular radio personalities in the country.

As the top-rated morning DJ at KIIS in Los Angeles, Dees spins what he calls "the best hits of the eight-dees and nine-dees" sandwiched between improvisational humor, comedy bits, and character portrayals.

He also hosts a hugely successful "Weekly Top 40" countdown program, which is internationally syndicated.

But it's his clever sense of humor on his local show that attracts the most attention. For example, with his audience listening in, Dees called the hair-

PHOTO COURTESY: CD Media

dresser of First Lady Hillary Clinton in Washington and pretended to be the President. "The guy believed I was him!" recalled Dees. "I said, 'Look, bald-headed women turn me on, and Hillary and I love to play jokes on each other all the time . . . Would you just shave her head before she can say anything about it? . . . That would really turn me on. Would you do that?' And the guy said, 'Mr. Clinton, I'd do anything for you, but I don't know what to say!'"

Disco Duck

Went to a party the other night
All the ladies were treating me right
Movin' my feet to the disco beat
How in the world could I keep my seat

All of a sudden I began to change
I was on the dance floor acting strange
Flapping my arms I began to cluck
Look at me, I'm the disco duck

Oh get down mama
I've got to have me a mama

Disco disco duck
Disco disco duck
Try your luck
Don't be a cluck
Disco disco disco disco disco
Disco disco duck
Disco disco duck

Oh get down mama
Oh mama, shake your tailfeather

When the music stopped, I returned to
my seat
But there's no stopping the duck and
his beat
So I got back up to try my luck
Why look, everybody's doing the disco
duck

Disco disco duck
Disco disco duck
Try your luck
Don't be a cluck
Disco disco disco disco disco disco
Disco disco duck
Disco disco duck
Try your luck
Don't be a cluck
Disco disco disco disco disco disco
Disco disco duck
Disco disco duck
Try your luck
Don't be a cluck
Disco disco disco disco disco duck

MACARTHUR PARK
Richard Harris

#3

FOR THE RECORD

Released by Dunhill Records in 1968.
Playing time: 7:21.
Reached #2 on the *Billboard* Hot 100.

BACKGROUND MUSIC

If ever there was a love-it-or-hate-it song, it was "MacArthur Park." This forlorn, lengthy tune about lost love appealed to millions of listeners. But even more thought the song sucked big time.

Critics derided the record as "a loser about a loser," "a saccharine song," and "a wilted nosegay of music." Also pilloried were actor Richard Harris for a voice "that's like drilling on a nerve;" the production, which allegedly sounded "like 800 violins and a heavenly choir of 10,000 in an orgy of sickeningly sweet sentiment;" and the "greeting-card, surrealistic lyrics that make little sense."

The song has evoked such everlasting loathing that in 1993, when nationally-syndicated columnist Dave Barry asked his readers which songs they hated the most, "MacArthur Park" topped the list. That was 25 years after the record's initial release! (Donna Summer's disco version of the tune, which went all the way to #1 in 1978, probably had a good deal to do with the song's later notoriety.) Most

often cited for condemnation were the interminable length, Harris' singing, and the obscure lyrics, especially the bit about leaving the cake out in the rain.

The song, written by Jimmy Webb, was based on his personal experience of a relationship gone sour. Webb used to meet his girlfriend Susan for a picnic lunch at MacArthur Park, a 32-acre refuge for the old and aimless on the seedy fringe of downtown Los Angeles.

"It's really simple," Webb told record biz author Joe Smith. "You associate a place with a person. You spend a lot of time there with that person, and when the relationship ends, you do a lot of thinking about the place. That's what 'MacArthur Park' is all about. I used to go there and have lunch. That's where the cake comes from. The image is, the rain comes and the whole thing is going, or melting, and then it's gone."

Webb was a rising star in the music world. Fresh out of Oklahoma, the son of a Baptist minister moved to Los Angeles and, before his 21st birthday, had scored big by writing such hits as "Up, Up and Away," which won a Grammy, and "By the Time I Get To Phoenix."

At the time, he became friends with Irish-born film star Richard Harris, who invited Webb to Ireland where they traveled around and hit the pubs. Because Harris had just finished shooting the movie musical *Camelot* in which he starred as King Arthur, the two began talking about making a record together. Webb pulled out some of the songs he had written that had yet to be recorded and played them on a piano in Harris' London flat. One of the tunes was "MacArthur Park"—and the actor loved it. Even though Harris had never cut a single before, he eagerly wanted to record it.

"He went for it immediately," Webb recalled. "He must have had some kind of premonition. He fastened on that song and wanted to do it. At the time, I thought, 'Well how adventurous and ambitious of him.'"

NOTEWORTHY NOTES

- If you listen carefully, you will hear Richard Harris mistakenly call it "MacArthur's Park" throughout the song instead of "MacArthur Park." When a reporter informed him of the gaffe in 1968, Harris self-mockingly told himself, "Get it right next time, you fool."

- KHJ—the most influential rock radio station in Los Angeles at the time—refused to play the song unless it was edited down. Webb stood firm and told them to either air the entire record or don't play it at all. A week later, the station began playing "MacArthur Park."

- Although some stations hated playing such a long record, it was a godsend for many disc jockeys. While the song was on, they could go to the bathroom, call their girlfriends, or eat their pizza without rushing.

- Webb and Harris had a falling out after the song became a hit. The actor promised to give Webb his Rolls Royce if the record made it to the Top 10. After it reached #2, Harris offered Webb a different Rolls, but Webb wanted the one Harris had promised him. They had an argument and didn't speak to each other for years.

PLATTER PATTER

MacArthur Park" was originally the last movement in a 22-minute cantata that Jimmy Webb wanted the Association to record on their next album. But the group refused.

"Jimmy thought the Association would be perfect to record his cantata," recalled producer Bones Howe. "He wanted a whole side of their next album for the cantata, which could be broken up into pieces for singles.

"I set up a meeting with Jimmy

and the Association and he played the cantata for them on the piano. It was a wonderful piece of music. After he left, the group met with me and said, 'Any two guys in this group could write a better piece of music than that. We don't want to give up a whole side of our album. We're hot right now.'

"I said, 'You're crazy. This is a wonderful concept. This is an opportunity to go forward creatively and do something that nobody's done before.' They wouldn't do it and they left it to me to tell Jimmy. He was crushed."

Howe reluctantly agreed to produce the Association's next album, "Birthday"—but only after he told them they had made a big mistake.

"When 'MacArthur Park' first made it to the Top 10, I called up my attorney and told him to inform Warner Brothers that I wouldn't produce the Association anymore," said Howe.

The Association's LP bombed.

PHOTO COURTESY: Columbia Pictures

FOLLOW UPS AND DOWNS

Harris followed up "MacArthur Park" with three singles that failed to make the Top 40: "The Yard Went on Forever," #64 in 1968; "Didn't We," #63 in 1969; and "My Boy," #41 in 1972.

ROCK ON

When the market for melodramatic ballads dried up, Jimmy Webb moved to New Jersey where he raised a family and still composes music for movies, television and the theater.

Although Richard Harris' musical career took a nosedive, his acting didn't. He's starred in dozens of movies and appeared in the Oscar-winning *The Unforgiven* in 1992.

MacArthur Park

Spring was never waiting for us, girl
It ran one step ahead
As we followed in the dance.

Between the parted pages
And were pressed
In love's hot fevered iron
Like a striped pair of pants.

MacArthur Park is melting in the dark
All the sweet green icing flowing down.
Someone left the cake out in the rain
I don't think that I can take it
'Cause it took so long to bake it
And I'll never have that recipe again
Oh no.

I recall the yellow cotton dress
Foaming like a wave
On the ground around your knees.

The birds like tender babies
In your hands
And the old man playing checkers
by the trees.

MacArthur Park is melting in the dark
All the sweet green icing flowing down
Someone left the cake out in the rain
I don't think that I can take it
'Cause it took so long to bake it
And I'll never have that recipe again
Oh no.

There will be another song for me
For I will sing it
There will be another dream for me
Someone will bring it.

I will drink the wine
While it is warm
And never let you catch me
Looking at the sun
And after all the loves of my life
After all the loves of my life
You'll still be the one.

I will take my life into my hands
And I will use it
I will win the worship in their eyes
And I will lose it.

I will have the things that I desire
And my passion flow like rivers
    through the sky
And after all the loves of my life
Oh, after all the loves of my life
I'll be thinking of you
And wondering why.

MacArthur Park is melting in the dark
All the sweet green icing flowing down
Someone left the cake out in the rain
I don't think that I can take it
'Cause it took so long to bake it
And I'll never have that recipe again
Oh no, oh no
No, no, no, oh no.

YUMMY, YUMMY, YUMMY
Ohio Express

#2

FOR THE RECORD

Released by Buddah Records in 1968.
Playing time: 2:18.
Reached #4 on the *Billboard* Hot 100 as well as #4 on the charts in England.
Sold a million copies in two months.

BACKGROUND MUSIC

Although Ohio Express is credited with this inane bubblegum hit, the truth is the band didn't record one note of the song. What listeners heard was the demo by one of the tune's writers, backed by session musicians!

"Yummy, Yummy, Yummy" was composed by Joey Levine and Arthur Resnick who worked with Jerry Kasenetz and Jeff Katz, early pioneers of bubblegum music—commercially packaged songs aimed specifically at the pre-teen market.

Before breaking into the music business, Resnick, a graduate of Johns Hopkins University, was a traveling salesman who hated his work. "I kept getting fired," he recalled. "And I was spending my free time writing poetry. So for three years, I bummed around getting fired and writing poetry."

He was inspired to get into music by a friend, Barry Mann, who had written "You've Lost That Lovin' Feelin'" and "On Broadway." Resnick started writing songs and eventually co-wrote such hits as "Under the Boardwalk,"

"A Little Bit of Heaven," and "Sand in My Shoes."

Then he teamed up with teenage whiz Joey Levine, who was still attending college in New York and writing songs between classes. In addition to writing, Levine did vocals on many of the Kasenetz-Katz records, which, more often than not, were credited to rock groups that didn't really exist.

Levine and a studio session crew were the ones who recorded "Simon Says"—not the 1910 Fruitgum Company, which Kasenetz and Katz conjured up after noticing the moniker on a bubblegum wrapper. When the song became a hit, the producers decided to capitalize on other popular playground games and phrases. So Levine and session musicians went to the studio to record "May I Take a Giant Step," "1, 2, 3, Red Light," "Goody Goody Gumdrops," and "Indian Giver."

When these songs, too, became hits for the still nonexistent 1910 Fruitgum Company, the producers rounded up a group of rock musicians to become the band for the sole purpose of promoting the records on tour.

"I didn't like to tour, so I didn't go," recalled Levine. "I didn't mind being anonymous. I was having fun coming up with hit songs."

Levine and Resnick then wrote "Keep the Ball Rollin'" for Jay and the Techniques. "I couldn't stand that song," confessed Resnick. "I hated it so much. It was one of those stupid songs that we wrote.

"One day we were trying to find another stupid song that we could write and we were tossing titles back and forth." It just so happened that they were eating lunch at a Chinese restaurant called King Yum at the time. So Resnick came up with the title "Yummy," which Levine rejected at first.

"The next day," recalled Resnick, "Joey came back and said, 'Remember that title you had?' Then he started to play me 'Yummy, Yummy, Yummy.' We did a demo and took it to Jerry Ross, producer of Jay and the Techniques and he turned the song down. He hated it. He absolutely hated it.

That was understandable.

"So we took it to Kasenetz and Katz. As dumb a song as it was, the demo sounded good. They went nutso over it." The producers asked them to go back in the studio, fine-tune it, and record it as a demo for the group Ohio Express.

"We got a session crew together and I sang lead because the Ohio Express was out of town," recalled Levine. "The producers said that the group could learn the song when it got back. But when Neil Bogart [head of Buddah Records] heard the demo, he said, 'Get it out and put Ohio Express' name on the label, because it's great the way it is.'"

The first time Ohio Express heard "their" song was after the single had been released. Said guitarist Doug Grassel, "When we first heard it, it was such a different sound that we were looking at each other and saying, 'What?' And the producers said, 'Don't worry. Play this and you'll be stars.' So we did and that's what happened."

PLATTER PATTER

Ohio Express was formed in high school—as a way to pick up girls.

"We got together in school in Mansfield, Ohio, in 1965," said original member Doug Grassel. "We figured it was a nice way to pick up women." Fortunately, the teens could also play music; eventually they came to the attention of Kasenetz and Katz

in New York.

In 1967, under the guidance of the two producers, Ohio Express recorded "Beg, Borrow and Steal" which made it to #29. But although their biggest hit—"Yummy, Yummy, Yummy"—was one they never recorded, the group did make other lesser hits given to them by Kasenetz and Katz.

Michael Ochs Archives

"Those two were difficult to work with," said Grassel.

"It was strictly a money game with them. They'd tell us, 'Keep it simple. Hurry up. You're costing us money.' They'd tell us what songs to play. And if we told them we didn't like a particular song, they'd say something like, 'Who do you think you are? Jimi Hendrix?'"

FOLLOW UPS AND DOWNS

Ohio Express followed up "Yummy, Yummy, Yummy" with more bubblegum hits, including "Down at Lulu's," "Chewy Chewy" (the group's second-biggest hit at #15), "Sweeter than Sugar," and "Mercy."

ROCK ON

After a string of hits, Resnick and Levine left Kasenetz and Katz in 1970 when bubblegum music died out.

Levine joined a rock group called Reunion that had one hit, the strange "Life Is A Rock (But the Radio Rolled Me)." The song—a recitation in machine-gun delivery of some of the great artists, phrases, and titles in rock history—reached #8 in 1974.

Eventually, Levine drifted into the advertising business and Resnick, who continued to write songs for several years, retired.

Ohio Express still does gigs, playing at car shows, mall openings, and Wolfman Jack's oldies shows.

Yummy, Yummy, Yummy

Yummy, yummy, yummy
I got love in my tummy
And I feel like a-lovin' you
Love, you're such a sweet thing
Good enough to eat thing
And that's just a-what I'm gonna do.

Ooh love to hold ya
Ooh love to kiss ya
Ooh love, I love it so
Ooh love, you're sweeter
Sweeter than sugar
Ooh love, I won't let you go.

Yummy, yummy, yummy
I got love in my tummy
And as silly as it may seem
The lovin' that you're givin'
Is what keeps me livin'
And your love is like peaches and
*   cream.*

Kinda like sugar
Kinda like spices
Kinda like, like what you do
Kinda sounds funny
But love, honey
Honey, I love you.

Yummy, yummy, yummy
I got love in my tummy
That your love can satisfy
Love, you're such a sweet thing
Good enough to eat thing
And sweet thing, that ain't no lie.

I love to hold ya
Ooh love to kiss ya
Ooh love, I love it so
Ooh love, you're sweeter
Sweeter than sugar
Ooh love, I won't let you go.

THEY'RE COMING TO TAKE ME AWAY, HA-HAAA!

Napoleon XIV

FOR THE RECORD

Released by Warner Brothers Records in 1966.
Playing time: 2:10.
Peaked at #3 on the *Billboard* Hot 100.
Sold over half a million copies in one week.
Remained on the charts only six weeks before radio stations refused to play it because of its controversial subject matter.
Re-released in 1973 and reached #87.

BACKGROUND MUSIC

The hit song about a man who loses his mind when his beloved pooch leaves him was written by a former mental patient!

Nine years before Jerry Samuels (aka Napoleon XIV) wrote and recorded the wacky tune, he spent eight months in a psychiatric hospital. "It was a fascinating experience—very beneficial," recalled Samuels.

"We always made fun of ourselves. Later, when I did the record, I knew it wouldn't offend mental patients. They laughed at it. I would have laughed at it if I had heard it when I was in the hospital. It would have become the mental patients' theme song."

In 1965, when Samuels was a 27-year-old songwriter and recording engineer, he suddenly had an inspiration to write a tune about a madman. "It popped into my head and I thought it was funny," he recalled. "When I started to write it, I called some friends and they were hysterical.

"I wrote the first verse and chorus in a couple of hours and then I put it away for about three months. I wrote the second verse and chorus and then put it away for another six months."

As an afterthought, Samuels included a verse about why the man went insane—over his "mangy mutt" that had run off.

"I thought the dog verse helped take the edge off the song and make it even funnier," he said.

"When I finally finished writing it, I knew the song would be a big hit."

So he booked an hour and a half

of studio time. Then, with just a drum, a tambourine, and his own demented vocal stylings, Samuels recorded "They're Coming To Take Me Away, Ha-Haaa!"

"I needed a name for myself and a friend said, 'Hey, why don't you call yourself Napoleon?' I thought that was pretty good. My attorney suggested that I add something else to the name so I could trademark it. I picked XIV— Napoleon XIV—because I liked the way the Roman numerals looked together. There was no other reason."

When George Lee, an executive with Warner Brothers, heard Napoleon XIV's zany tune, he released it immediately. Sales of the record soared into the stratosphere—a half million records in less than one week! But mental health organizations raised a ruckus, claiming that the song made fun of the mentally ill. As a result, stations pulled the record from their playlists.

NOTEWORTHY NOTES

- The music was inspired by a Scottish tune called "The Campbells Are Coming."

- It cost Samuels $30 to record the song—$25 for the recording tape and a $5 rental fee for a hand-cranked siren used near the end of the song.

- The song was the fastest-selling record in Warner Brothers history.

- Tiny Tim recorded a disco version of "They're Coming To Take Me Away, Ha-Haaa!" but it failed to make the charts.

- Samuel's hit is the only Top 40 single to feature the same song recorded *backwards* on the "B" side. Even the flip side title is reversed.

PLATTER PATTER

As Napoleon XIV, Jerry Samuels performed "They're Coming To Take Me Away, Ha-Haaa!" only *once* in public.

"The first and only time that I sang the song in front of a live audience, I felt I was being laughed at," Samuels revealed. "That was very hard for me to take.

"My wife was in the audience of 2,000 kids and she overheard someone say, 'Hey, would you look at that yo-yo?' I got off that stage very quickly and I never performed that song again. I wanted no part of doing it live anymore."

Because Napoleon XIV sang while wearing a mask, Samuels' agent secretly hired another singer to play the part. Said Samuels, "It was like a Milli Vanilli thing."

FOLLOW UPS AND DOWNS

Follow-up songs by Napoleon XIV that unfortunately, but understandably, bombed included:

"They're Coming To Get Me Again, Ha-Haaa!"

"I Live in a Split-Level Head"

"Marching Off to Bedlam"

"I'm in Love with My Little Red Tricycle"

ROCK ON

Jerry Samuels owns and operates a Philadelphia talent agency that caters to senior citizen facilities. He represents about 140 entertainers who perform at over 400 centers for the elderly. The slogan of the Jerry Samuels Agency is "Entertaining the Young at Heart."

Michael Ochs Archives

They're Coming to Take Me Away, Ha-Haaa!

Remember when you ran away
And I got on my knees
And begged you not to leave
Because I'd go beserk.

Well you left me anyhow
And then the days got worse and worse
And now you see I've gone
Completely out of my mind.

And they're coming to take me away,
*   ha-haaa*
They're coming to take me away, ho-ho
Hee-hee, ha-ha, to the funny farm
Where life is beautiful all the time
And I'll be happy to see those nice
*   young men*
In their clean white coats
And they're coming to take me away,
*   ha-haaa!*

You thought it was a joke
And so you laughed
You laughed when I said
That losing you would make me flip
*   my lid.*

Right? You know you laughed
I heard you laugh. You laughed
You laughed and laughed and then
*   you left*
But now you know I'm utterly mad.

And they're coming to take me away,
*   ha-haaa*
They're coming to take me away,
*   ho-ho, hee-hee, ha-haaa*
To the happy home with trees and flowers
And chirping birds and basket
*   weavers who sit and smile*
And twiddle their thumbs and toes
And they're coming to take me away,
*   ha-haaa!*

I cooked your food
I cleaned your house
And this is how you pay me back
For all my kind unselfish, loving deeds.
Ha! Well you just wait
They'll find you yet and when they do
They'll put you in the A.S.P.C.A.
You mangy mutt.

And they're coming to take me away,
*   ha-haaa*
They're coming to take me away,
*   ha-haaa, ho-ho, hee-hee*
To the funny farm where life is
*   beautiful all the time*
And I'll be happy to see those nice
*   young men*
In their clean white coats

And they're coming to take me away,
*   ha-haaa*
To the happy home with trees and
*   flowers*
And chirping birds and basket
*   weavers who sit and smile*
And twiddle their thumbs and toes
And they're coming to take me away,
*   ha-haaa!*

Credits

ESCAPE (THE PIÑA COLADA SONG). Words and Music by Rupert Holmes. ©1979 WB MUSIC CORP. & THE HOLMES LINE OF MUSIC, INC. All rights administered by WB MUSIC CORP. All Rights Reserved.

THE HOMECOMING QUEEN'S GOT A GUN. Words & Music by Ray Colcord, Terrence McNally, Julie Brown and Charlie Coffey. Copyright ©1984 Stymie Music, Bitchen Tunes and Charlie Coffey Music. Used by Permission. All Rights Reserved.

I'M HENERY THE EIGHTH, I AM. Words & Music by Murray & Weston.

ITSY BITSY TEENIE WEENIE YELLOW POLKA DOT BIKINI. Words & Music by Paul Vance & Lee Pockriss. Copyright ©1960 (Renewed) by Music Sales Corporation (ASCAP) and Emily Music Corp. International Copyright Secured. All Rights Reserved. Reprinted by Permission.

JUNK FOOD JUNKIE. Words & Music by Larry Groce. Copyright ©1974, 1976 Peaceable Kingdom Music Publishing. Used by Permission. All Rights Reserved.

KOOKIE, KOOKIE (LEND ME YOUR COMB). Words & Music by Irving Taylor. Copyright ©1959 Warner Bros. Inc. (Renewed). Used by Permission. All Rights Reserved.

LOUIE, LOUIE. Words & Music by Richard Berry. Copyright ©1967 Windswept Pacific Entertainment Co. DBA Longitude Music Co. Used by Permission. All Rights Reserved.

MACARTHUR PARK. Words and Music by Jimmy Webb. Copyright ©1968 Canopy Music, Inc. All Rights Administered by Polygram International Publishing Inc. International Copyright Secured. All Rights Reserved.

MR. CUSTER. Words and Music by Fred Darian, Al DeLory and Joe VanWinkle. Copyright ©1960 (Renewed 1988) Pattern Music, Inc. All Rights Administered by All Nations Music. International Copyright Secured. All Rights Reserved.

MONSTER MASH. Lyrics of the song MONSTER MASH reprinted herein are Copyright ©1962, 1973 by Gary S. Paxton Music, Inc., Acoustic Music, Inc. and Capizzi Music Co. 1962 Copyright Renewed. All rights administered by Acoustic Music, Inc., P.O. Box 210317, Nashville, TN 37221. International Copyright Secured. All Rights Reserved. Reprinted by Permission.

Index

About the Authors

BRUCE NASH and ALLAN ZULLO are the authors of the Hall of Shame series of books. Mr. Nash lives in Burbank, California; Mr. Zullo lives in Palm Beach Gardens, Florida.